T0380930

Missing Something?

Johnny Doubter

Archway Publishing books may be ordered through booksellers or by contacting:

Archway Publishing
1663 Liberty Drive
Bloomington, IN 47403
www.archwaypublishing.com
844-669-3957

ISBN: 978-1-6657-0901-9 (sc)
ISBN: 978-1-6657-0902-6 (hc)
ISBN: 978-1-6657-0903-3 (e)

Library of Congress Control Number: 2021913328

Print information available on the last page.

Archway Publishing rev. date: 7/30/2021

INTRODUCTION

This book is heavy on science, challenging on religion, light on humor (but not completely lacking) with much life in-between. Life experiences from my 76 years includes philosophy, poetry and other thought provoking stuff.

Have you ever wanted to ask "Why?" Children ask why over and over, and eventually the answer comes back "well that is just how it is." Scientists might say "the current theory is this or that". I think we find out at a very young age that there are many things we just need to accept and move on. Unfortunate! What gullible fools we become! We have huge brains and we allow them to go to sleep, unfulfilled much of the time. From birth we are surrounded by experts and we are taught to follow what they tell us. Yet nothing new will ever be discovered if we just follow. I am not disregarding the value of parents, teachers and professionals, but knowledge cannot be advanced if we never take it to the next level. We all have one of our own powerful and incomprehensible computers stuck between our ears, but if we believe it is empty until filled by someone else we will never advance human understanding. Why aren't we be taught to keep challenging, study thoroughly what is being thrown at us, consume what is good and add whatever we can to create a deeper and richer comprehension? In other words "**Dig Deeper**." We all have the capability and are naturally evolved investigators, but we have been foolishly convinced that we are consumers and our job is to digest whatever the "experts" provide. We have a right and responsibility to awaken that sleepy organ snoozing in our heads. Don't place it in neutral just because you believe that what you think doesn't matter. Curiosity has changed how we perceive the universe forever.

So get off of your duff and start changing this world. You must challenge the rampant folly that masquerades as common knowledge or established hypotheses. I am convinced that this world is full of people just like you who have the ability to discover and share many new and amazing things, but you just don't feel worthy, or significant, or educated enough to share them! I refuse to continue to be one of those people and you should too!

I have no college degree and my mathematic skills are miniscule. Except for supporting drawings, charts and data, I will attempt to keep math out of this book. If some things in this book seem too deep, too ridiculous or uninteresting for you, just skip them. What makes all of us great is our differences. This is a colorful world and your color is needed to complete a comprehensive picture. Don't let your paint dry out before it is included within our human story.

Being a somewhat plain nobody is very convenient for me. I have no reputation to lose, but if any of the principles herein are worthy of discussion or expansion, just maybe minds will be opened and something good will come of it. Something may catch your fancy and you may even gain enough confidence to share some world changing ideas of your own.

Much of what this book contains are concepts that I developed years ago, some as far back as 50+ years. Many times I built equipment and experimented. My problem is this world contains far too many interesting and fun things so as soon as my curiosity is satisfied I set one thing aside and go on to whatever captures my fancy next. Now I am old and some things seem far too important to die with me. I hope I can finish this book before everything sinks into senility.

What a wonderful lush environment when these giant trees lived in Arizona

[Petrified Forest National Park]

CONTENTS

1. GLOBAL WARMING JUST IN TIME, OR MAYBE NOT!

When I first started hearing about global warming I was very uncomfortable because I was missing a lot of information. I knew that the earth had vastly more CO_2 in the beginning (possibly just under 100%). I also knew that there were time periods when the earth was much warmer and during some of those times plant and animal life was prolific covering nearly the entire earth. Therefore I needed to do more research to discover the truth. I suspected that an incredible "Inconvenient perversion" may be misleading all of humanity.

Consider this. Everything living is made of hydrocarbons. Indeed, you and I are carbon based organisms. Where do you think all the carbon came from that makes up our bodies as well as every living thing? Every carbon atom within every living organism came out of our original atmosphere and upper levels of the oceans. Abundant CO_2 is dominant in young planetary atmospheres that have no living organisms to consume it.

Almost everyone knows the process for common life; plants take in water (H_2O), carbon dioxide (CO_2) and energy from the sun. Then through the process of photosynthesis plant life creates sugars/hydrocarbons for building plant structures, releasing the oxygen in the process. We exclusively eat, and are made of these hydrocarbons! Without CO_2 in our atmosphere and oceans, **life on earth would not exist** (*with possible extremophile exceptions*).

Some scientists speculate that earth's original atmosphere may have had CO_2 percentages much like Mars is today, about 96% CO_2, or Venus at 96.5% CO_2. [*On earth the presence of nitrogen could dilute that number, but no one knows when or how our nitrogen arrived.*] Most scientist agree that atmospheric CO_2 was exponentially higher during the young developing earth and it was much warmer and wetter with vigorous ocean water evaporation. However, when photosynthetic (plant) life began it started consuming our CO_2 and releasing oxygen. As a result, today we have an **exceptionally low .04% of atmospheric CO_2 remaining** and a comparatively dry environment.

While most of humanity stresses out over global warming and the extremely modest human caused CO_2 increases, I wonder how plants have continued to adapt, even survive, after using up nearly all of earth's atmospheric CO_2. CO_2 is what plants breathe. Plants have been shown to grow much better in an augmented CO_2 environment and specialty growers are finding growth advantages by raising the level of CO_2 within greenhouses. I suggest that plant growth increases are an indicator of how much stress plants are in from the continual and almost complete depletion of earth's CO_2. I believe that photosynthetic organisms that developed early were much more prolific and energetic, growing at a much faster metabolic rate during earth's early years, inefficiently consuming abundant amounts of CO_2. After life attained a strong foothold, CO_2 started to be vigorously consumed culminating at about 716 million years ago when this rapid CO_2 depletion may have cooled earth until it became what is called a "snowball earth." This was a time when earth was almost completely frozen all the way to the equator. The highly energetic photosynthetic organisms that needed high levels of CO_2 probably died off at that time due to "suffocation" from a lack of sufficient CO_2. The slower rate of photosynthetic growth that we observe today was probably an evolutionary adaption of remaining organisms to the continually diminishing levels of CO_2.

So where did all that life giving essential CO_2 end up? The remains of living organisms are stored underground in vast hydrocarbon deposits of oil, gas and coal. Additionally, layers of calcifying organism deposits including shell, coral and other plankton sediments have been cemented together and turned into rock, storing the carbon in limestone (mostly <u>calcium carbonate</u> ($CaCO_3$) and its derivatives). So the result of eons of deposits from living organisms has almost completely locked up most of the CO_2 taken from our biosphere. This CO_2 reduction has inevitably led to a cooling and drying environment throughout our entire planet. We know that over 20% of our atmosphere is oxygen produced exclusively by photosynthesis. You could calculate how much CO_2 might be locked up in deposits if you are so inclined, but you would also need to know how much oxygen is locked up in iron oxides. Try calculating if you like, but I have lost interest already.

Let's summarize what has been stated so far. Plant life photosynthesis has removed the vast majority of CO_2 from our biosphere and stored it underground and under the ocean within various deposits, and plants cannot live without CO_2. Therefore, neither can you or I. Consider our dry lakes and previous ice encroachments. Call them ice ages or glacial periods. It is reasonable to believe these recurring cooling and drying periods have occurred primarily due to the relentless reduction of CO_2. Wake up people! Look around! What do you see? Deserts are advancing and lakes are drying up everywhere. My house is located within a dry lakebed. The meager increases of CO_2 from our industrial revolution has affected the environment very little so far. This is understandable since an increase of 200 ppm is like adding $1^2/_3$ ounces of water into a full 55 gallon drum. If the drum was empty I doubt this would even wet the entire bottom.

I do not deny "global warming", but I propose a position unlike most. I believe that the current warming trend is occurring, and I say **"great, this is exactly what we need!"** I disagree with some things that have been stated like "deserts will spread." People who say this want to have their bad news both ways. How can you have more evaporation from warming oceans resulting in more rain and more deserts at the same time? I know, some places will get dryer for a time, but as you will see these will be temporary adjustments to a temporary change. The atmosphere heats first and then it heats the oceans which takes much longer. We cannot ignore the added evaporation from the warming of ocean water. In a time when Earth was much warmer, rivers even ran through the Sahara Desert and herds of huge dinosaurs had plenty to eat and drink in the Americas. Since the atmosphere warms up very fast compared to the heat-sinking properties of our vast oceans, today's intermediate condition in no way represents the eventual positive end results that <u>could</u> occur from a warming planet. The common belief is that the oceans will become more saline. I am not an expert, but I also question this since most of the melting ice contains fresh water. Added carbon might increase acidity, but that has happened many times before in past ages and living organisms have adapted. Has the effects of increased solar reflection from the additional bright reflective cloud cover been considered as a mitigating variable?

When I was a young man 60 + years ago the big question was, considering the history of recurring ice ages [glacial periods], are we heading back into one? This was a serious concern at that time since we knew nothing about greenhouse gasses or potential global warming in those days. Humanity (as we know it) would not survive this cold and disastrous possibility! Fertile land for growing our food would be drastically reduced. I wondered why there has been such a dramatic reversal of thinking and I wanted to know the rest of the story.

During the last **glacial** *maximum about 20,000 years ago, much of the world was cold, dry, and inhospitable, with frequent storms and a dust-laden atmosphere. Massive sheets of ice locked away water, lowering the sea level, exposing continental shelves, joining land masses together, and creating extensive coastal plains. Vast ice sheets covered much of North America, northern Europe, and Asia. The ice sheets profoundly affected Earth's climate by causing drought, desertification, and a dramatic drop in sea levels.* **Source - https:// en.wikipedia.org/wiki/Last_Glacial_Maximum.** [Producing food in the way and amount that we do today would be impossible.] (*My addition*)

Disclaimer

The following Figures (Charts and Graphs) are carefully drawn and closely represent what has been scientifically determined. Data charts derived from ice core analysis are available on the internet for your comparison and I recommend you do your own research, especially as newer research becomes available.

Let's take a look at this first chart. This chart is rich in pertinent information and covers the last 550 million years representing a small more recent piece of earths 4.7 billion year history. I presume that if we could gain data from earth's beginning we would discover the initial CO_2 percentage to be well within the 90% - 100% range, very much like our neighboring planets. Refer to FIGURE 1 below:

Even though and Figures 1&2 contain the best current thinking, because of the great distance in time they also contains the largest potential uncertainty. Use these charts as best informed approximations.

Figure 1

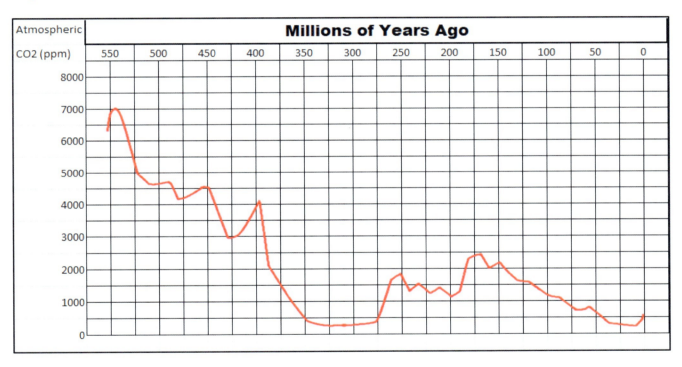

Figure 1 plots approximate atmospheric CO_2 levels and Figure 2 below plots the average global temperature over the same 550 million years. The left scale of figure 1 ranges from 0 to 8000 parts per million (ppm) of CO_2. (8000 ppm would be .8%), so by 550 million years ago earth's CO_2 had already been depleted to less than 1%. Follow the red CO_2 line which starts close to .65%, raises to .7%, and then diminishes to less than .1% around 300 million years ago. After that it jumps back up twice to about .25% and starts a slow decline toward today's level of about .04%. Compare this chart to many others available on the internet for possible updated data.

Observation:

Within the last 600 million years CO_2 levels have been astonishingly far above today's miniscule level for the majority of that time.

Figure 2

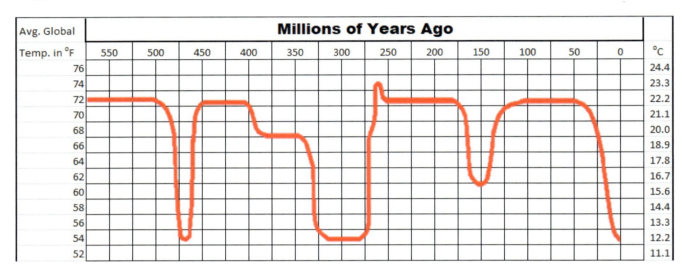

Figure 2 shows average global temperature over the same time period as Figure 1. The red line indicates temperature fluctuations between 53°F and 73°F. Remember, this is an average for everywhere on earth, poles to equator. There is one notable anomaly at about 470 million years ago (MYA). Temperature drops to ice age levels when CO_2 is still about 10 times today's level. What could have caused this? There are many possibilities, but no clear answers.

Some scientists believe that we have been, and are **right now,** in an overall Ice age that began near the middle of the Tertiary period (about 40 MYA). Observe the right most temperature drop of figure 2 line (above) that begins dropping from about 22°C to about 12°C during the last 40 million years. **This places us right now in an overall ice age**. Also see Ice Ages depicted in Figure 3 below:

Figure 3

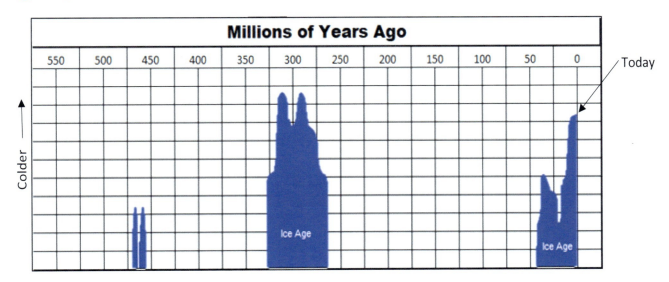

You will see in a later chart that expands time closer to today that the Ice age we are currently in contains cycles between long **glacial periods** (icy and very cold) and shorter **inter-glacial periods** (Reasonably comfortable for human life and activity).

Because previous Figures 1-3 graph 600 million years of time, fine details cannot be discerned within them. Therefore for more relevant data we must examine an additional expanded time chart. We will refer back to Figure 2 later to discover something extremely profound. Before we leave Figures 1-3 however, let's familiarize ourselves with significant observations. From about 175 million years ago to the present the CO_2 level has been continually reduced (allegedly) through the constant consumption of living organisms (photosynthesis and calcification) changing from a little over .2% to today's .04% (approximately 400 ppm & rising). If you follow the red line through time on these charts you will also see a somewhat irregular relationship between cold periods and the reduction of CO_2. Although there are obviously other unidentified factors involved such as volcanism and plate tectonics, the general trend is unquestionable. CO_2 and temperature generally track together. However, significant questions remain because you can find charted areas in Figures 1 & 2 when CO_2 was relatively low and temperature was very high and it lasted this way for millions of years. The opposite is also true.

Way before the beginning of this these charts when earth began approximately 4.7 billion years ago, earth's atmosphere was likely over 90% CO_2 (or possibly over 25% depending on when nitrogen arrived). Near the beginning of Figure 1, 550 million years ago (observe the line again) CO_2 had fallen to around .5% (5000 ppm). At this time it takes a sharp rise to about .7% (that would be over 17 times today's level). Got it?

Now, with this time scale clear in our minds, let's take a look at another chart that expands our more recent **450 thousand** years (that's just a sliver of time at the end of Figures 1-3). Refer to Figure 4: Remember; this figure spreads time within the last portion of our current "ice age" and displays the cycling between glacial (very cold) and inter-glacial (somewhat warm) periods like today. One more time, this figure expands a very narrow slice of time at the very end of the Tertiary period displaying only the last 450 thousand years within our current "ice age." [Boxes and arrows add clarification]

Figure 4

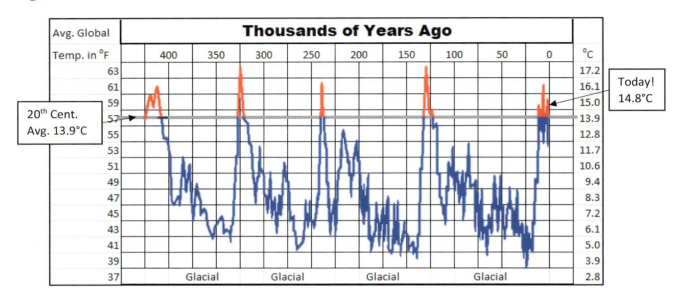

Red lines are inter-glacial warm periods (comfortable human living) and blue lines are cold to very cold glacial periods.

Glacial periods severely affect all life on earth. You can see five inter-glacial (warmer) periods (red lines including today) intermixed with four glacial periods (blue and very icy). The latest glacial episode was most intense near its end about 21,000 years ago, when glaciers covered almost the entire state of New York. In New York City, the Wisconsin Ice Sheet was about 1,000 feet thick. It is unnecessary to describe the impact that this would have if this were to even to begin to repeat today. I don't believe anyone knows the cause of these cycles between cold glacial and warm inter-glacial periods, but I will provide a guess at the conclusion of this section. It might be something yet to be discovered, but look carefully where we are today and the conditions across this Figure 4 chart. Compared to the other inter-glacial warm periods, the current amount of time above the 20th century reference line appears to have already lasted about as long, or longer, than previous warm periods before a rapid fall back into a glacial period occurs. I know that it is possible that we could have observed a slight warming period due to a human generated increase in CO_2, but has it been enough to avoid the next fall into a glacial disaster period? Consider the so-called "little ice age", a cool period between the years 1300 and 1870 that caused major disruptions in human activities and food production; and this was just a tiny temperature blip. Could this have been a forerunner of things to come? Also observe on Figure 4 how today we are well within the ups and downs of previous inter-glacial temperature variations where much higher temperature peaks have occurred than the warming we are currently experiencing. I propose that the current warming is **just as likely to be within an "inter-glacial normal" and not necessarily human induced**. Observe that all previous inter-glacial warm periods have a sharp rise in temperature just before falling back into a glacial deep freeze.

If we have the courage to look into the future, there could be an even greater danger. If our planet to reverses toward cooling and drying we might be on the edge of another "snowball earth" cliff. Scientists tell us that our planet experienced a "snowball earth" somewhat before 650 million years ago (before the beginning edge of our first charts). At that time the earth was believed to have frozen all the way to the equator calling into question how any living thing could have survived other than a few chemosynthesis extremophiles. How can we know that we are not dangerously close to another snowball earth tipping point? Observe figure 4 again. Each successive glacial period has gotten colder and longer than the previous ones. This might be because of progressive CO_2 depletion. If we were to enter another glacial period the bright reflective advancing ice just might reflect enough solar radiation back into space to pass the point of a snowball earth no return. Without considerably increasing CO_2 earth could be flirting with this disastrous possibility. No one knows what events got us out of the previous "snowball earth" condition(s). It could have been something catastrophic like massive volcanic activity that spread dark soot worldwide reversing the reflective properties of the ice and at the same time releasing massive amounts of CO_2 back into the atmosphere. What ever happened, the warming that followed brought on an explosion of new life forms (including what is known as the Cambrian Explosion).

For another quick review, all data shows, and most scientists agree, that we are currently in an ice age that started about 40 MYA and that we have been in a warm inter-glacial period within that ice age for about the last 10,000 years as shown in figure 4. The last glacial period lasted about 80,000 very icy years. Pay attention here! **Historically, it does not appear that inter-glacial warm periods last longer than the one we are currently in!**

Now let's return and look at something very interesting on the first charts (Figures 1&2). Throughout the duration of chart 2, the global average temperature seems to top out at about 22^0C (71.6^0F) no matter how high atmospheric CO_2 gets!!! Follow the lines again through the entire 600 million years. It seems that something is stopping earth from heating higher than 22^0C; and guess what, this temperature is where life of all kinds flourishes. I call this heating termination point the "Oceanic Evaporation Equilibrium Temperature." I believe that at a global temperature of 22^0C the increased evaporation of ocean water creates enough cloud cover to reflect sufficient solar energy back into space to stop further heating. The amount of energy absorbed by earth becomes equal to the amount reflected back into space. This produces a very lush, rainforest like environment all the way from the equator to the poles. The thick cloud cover from evaporation moderates temperatures throughout the planet. Consider this: What happens when it is cloudy? Commonly daytime is cooler since sunshine is blocked and nights are warmer when thermal radiation is reflected back toward earth. Clouds act as both a reflector of heat in the day and a blanket holding it in at night. Because of a much higher cloud cover than today's 40%, temperature would moderate throughout the entire earth, poles to equator. For humans 22^0C, which is 71.6^0F would open up great areas of habitable land, and for plants, clouds produce nurturing rain and pass the UV rays they need for photosynthesis. During such past ages, there were lakes and rivers everywhere. Crocodile fossils have been found near the poles. I believe attaining this temperature should be the goal of humanity and we should do everything possible to return our earth back into this Eden like equilibrium zone. Think about it. The sun is most direct and hottest at the equator year around. By conventional wisdom it should contain the most deserts. However, instead you find the most rainforests and lush jungles. Water evaporation and natural recycling through rain creates amazing things. Heavy cloud cover would reduce temperature variations that contribute to violent storms caused by intensely different atmospheric temperatures and pressures. During such past ages North America was Warm (about 71.60F), lush and supported large animal herds of all kinds, even mastodons. Plant life was so prolific that there was enough food to support 120 foot 80 ton dinosaurs.

Surely this would take more time than any of us have living today, so I am not ready to invest in Siberian real estate or abandon my dry lake bed home quite yet. Change will come slowly, but with a continued global multi-generational effort, and if we can accelerate our current warming trend, earth might be saved from a very cold, dry and possibly permanent death!

My fear is this. There is so much carbon stored within earth's crust that even a massive human effort could only recover even a tiny percentage for release back into the atmosphere. We would have to create a multitude of massive machines to put more than a small dent in the earth's hydrocarbon and carbonate deposits.

Here is something else to consider. Figure 4 shows a fairly regular cycling between glacial and inter-glacial periods. I speculated about some sort of hysteresis effect. [I use this term liberally to mean a delayed or out of phase condition that stimulates an oscillation.] I wondered what might be causing these oscillations. After ruling out CO_2, I considered the frozen Methane at the bottom of oceans and within frozen bogs.

As a greenhouse gas, Methane has been determined to be 21 times more powerful than CO_2. If this is true things might even be ready to heat up faster. At this writing, Methane is >1800 parts per billion (ppb) and although this is still lower than CO_2 it might become enough to be the main contributor. Throughout known history Methane has existed at about 300 ppb. Consider the consequence of thawing of frozen Methane deposits until they are completely depleted and mixed within our atmosphere.

It is not enough to say CO_2 is increasing and this is damaging our planet without scientifically studying all aspects of our changing temperature phenomena. The current warming might save us from disaster or be a common predecessor to the next glacial period. We must know for sure!

Let's consider some final points. I believe that without the recent, somewhat tiny, human-caused rise in temperature we could be sliding past the edge of another snowball earth cliff. Look again at figure 4. Each successive glacial period gets a little colder. A more probable scenario still exists that we could be near the end of our inter-glacial warm period and heading toward another glacial period. We might still be traveling in that direction if this current warming trend turns out to be short lived! The highest risk to humans is to reenter a glacial period when most of our food producing land will become covered in thick ice! The sharp points at the temperature peaks in Figure 4 may indicate a relative fast reversal from warming, then plunging rapidly toward ice. We cannot become complacent that we are warming and going in the right direction. Observe how quickly things reverse toward cold after the highest peaks of previous inter-glacial periods.

Adequate human intellect and computing power needs to be redirected toward developing an intentional and robust atmospheric CO_2 return rate to bring our atmosphere up to a predetermined, appropriate and sustainable level, if this is even possible. Scientists need to define a plant and animal ideal living norm for the ratio between CO_2 and other atmospheric gasses like oxygen. Methods must be developed to attain and maintain a proper balance that will return our earth to the lush, CO_2 rich, life friendly planet it was about 100 million years ago with abundant fresh water for every living organism. Let's stop spending valuable resources toward considering how we can make Mars habitable and do some real research on what we need to do to bring earth back to a warm, moist, tropical like place full of prolific life all the way to the poles. I believe this can be done if we put enough brainpower together. I know, Mars is already rich in CO_2 and it may be easy to terraform, especially since there are no people to get in the way. We might even consider cooling Venus which could be easier, although the thick atmosphere would be crushing. Maybe there are mountains high enough for human survival after the installation of solar shielding, oxygen production and the caustics are dealt with. I don't know, but this is not attainable now.

Now, humans must learn to work together globally, creating the jobs that will be required to deal with the side effects of warming that are certain to affect many human lives. An extraordinary amount of work will be required to counter sea level rise, more violent storms (in the short term) and the eventual rehydrating of dry places. Just because a lot of us have elected to live in perilous places cannot remain justification to shirk our human intellectual responsibilities. We must attempt to take control of all essential factors and the ramifications of earth's changing atmosphere.

Don't get me wrong; I loathe poisonous pollutants and the EPA has a list of 187 of them (when this was writtens). CO_2 is not on the list because CO_2 is not a pollutant and has, in earth's past, been a significantly greater percentage of our atmosphere. CO_2 is absolutely essential for sustaining life. We are the only species on earth that might consciously reverse our inevitable slide toward another cold and dry disaster, but take heart; we may have unintentionally had a great (though feeble) start through our burning of hydrocarbons (gas, oil and coal). We must **not** stop now and we must begin to look at this issue through new and comprehensive scientific eyes. To tax anyone for releasing CO_2 into the atmosphere or to propose the burial of it are two of the most ludicrous and counterproductive suggestions I could ever imagine!

So let's stop considering CO_2 our enemy. It is an essential gas that mankind should control, but I believe at a much higher level than it exists in our atmosphere today for the good of all life on earth and to keep earth within a very safe, even prolific, food producing environment. I must say that my dream of a lush pole to equator rainforest earth may not be within the ability of mankind to attain, and there is little hope that even the first steps will occur within any of our lifetimes, but I believe that a change in attitude must begin now. In fact, it may be nearly impossible to achieve significant progress as plankton and other photosynthetic organisms start increasing metabolic activity and consuming higher levels of CO_2 in response to our feeble efforts, but doing the wrong thing is a mistake that could become terminal! Let's wake up and start using our intellectual and financial resources wisely!

Afterthought:

After completing this study I have renewed my theories concerning the evolution of a planetary body within a "Goldilocks" zone. After a planet cools from bombardment, water has formed on the surface and a thick CO_2 atmosphere exists, conditions for life may become right. Discounting chemosynthesis extremophiles, photosynthetic life somehow begins. At first organisms rapidly consume CO_2, H_2O and sunlight releasing oxygen and building hydrocarbons (sugars). Over eons this process reduces the level of CO_2 in the atmosphere and increases other gasses. As CO_2 diminishes, the photosynthetic lifeforms evolve to live on lower and lower levels of CO_2. Now if animal consumers (like us) do not evolve to live on the released oxygen and newly available hydrocarbons, the planet will continue to cool until all life stops and the planet ices over completely, essentially becoming a "Dead Planet." However, if animal like life forms develop soon enough, and eventually become smart enough to intentionally return enough CO_2 back into the atmosphere, life may continue. A balanced CO_2 and oxygen consumption may extend life indefinitely on a planet if completely controlled. Obviously, this is ridiculously simple, but it still may have a little merit.

We might want to thank God for the nitrogen, because without it to dilute the oxygen everything might have burned up long ago.

Summary and Conclusions:

- We have observed the cycles between cold glacial periods and warmer inter-glacial periods over the last 450 thousand years. By observing previous warm periods we can see that we have been in this warm period for about as long as warm periods last before falling back into a glacial period. We have also seen that each glacial period appears to be getting colder than the previous (Figure 4)
- Our current rising temperature remains well within the range of typical inter-glacial warm period ups and downs. Temperature may need to increase another 2°C + to exceed the highest peaks of some previous warm periods. Therefore, we cannot feel comfortable that another glacial period threat

has passed, and maybe not even after we exceed another 2°C higher. These temperature variations appear to be normal within interglacial periods

- Falling back into a glacial period would be catastrophic in comparison to continued warming (refer to "Little Ice Age" effects from 1300 and 1870). We must reduce this likelihood as much as possible by cleanly burning all fossil fuels that we can burn. However, I have no idea what can be done about all the carbon stored in solid rock.

- We have been in an overall ice age for about the last 40 million years (Figure 3). Compared to prehistoric CO_2 levels the tiny increase caused by humans will do very little to change this, but it <u>may</u> have started us toward reducing the chance of falling into another completely iced over planet. The continued release of CO_2 into our atmosphere is the best and only chance that we have for continued human advancement. [*Personally, I doubt we can do enough since so much carbon is tied up in hard deposits!*]

- The cause of the oscillations between inter-glacial warm periods and glacial cold periods is unknown and requires additional scientific study. Only dedicated analysis has a chance of determining the root cause(s) for these changing temperature oscillations in order to make informed decisions and do the right thing to preserve our future earth home. Below is one possible scenario:

  - I believe that oscillations between glacial and inter-glacial periods may be caused by a huge out-of-phase relationship between a rapidly changing atmosphere and the very slow heat sinking thermal properties of the ocean. It is easy to summarize such a relationship, but there are probably hundreds of unidentified variables involved. I will attempt to identify possible factors that could be contributors in order to propose a potentially viable oscillating wave progression illustrated in the following scenario:

One Possibility

1. Warming begins [cycling From item 9 below]. This starts an approximate 10 thousand year relatively warm intermediate period within the current ice age

1. Biological activity starts increasing methane within the atmosphere. Most methane is stored frozen at the bottom of the oceans and in bogs until earth heating reaches a tipping point where the methane starts to thaw and is rapidly released into the atmosphere. Methane begins to thaw first where it is exposed to the atmosphere followed eventually by the oceans as they slowly warm. **Methane** by weight has 21 times the global warming potential of carbon dioxide. As it builds in the atmosphere it this causes a rapid increase in global temperature that eventually overshoots >2°C (refer to Figure 4 peak temperatures) In some dryer and warmer places, forest fires increase, releasing soot and smoke which absorbs the sun's energy accelerating atmospheric heating

2. Oceans start to warm slowly in response to the heated atmosphere, but in response to the ocean warming, evaporation and increased rain, lakes and rivers begin covering the land. Humidity increases and cloud cover climbs from 40% (today) to something under 100%

3. Cloud cover starts to reflect almost all solar energy back into space terminating further heating of earth

4. Cloud cover remains high while surface temperatures start to fall

5. The global temperature starts to drop and form surface ice. Methane starts to refreeze out of the atmosphere

6. Frost, snow and ice start to reflect solar energy replacing cloud cover which is diminishing. This cloud to ice transition overshoots and continues to reduce atmospheric temperature as the oceans also begin cooling

7. The earth enters another glacial period (or worse a snowball earth) with the surface completely frozen, and highly reflective, even as clouds disappear. This glacial period may last 80 thousand years or more

8. Eventually, volcanic activity, wind and space debris starts to contaminate the reflective icy surface with soot, ash and dust allowing the surface to again start absorbing solar energy

9. An inter-glacial worming period begins again, possibly after reaching another heating trip point. Return to #1 (Above).

o So challenge me, "This is far too simple and there must be many other interacting factors", but this just might stimulate a more productive and comprehensive analysis.

o Additional questions:

- Why isn't the recovery from cold more irregular (in time) if it is purely dependent on irregular tectonic activity?

- Could the warm period have been sustained if human activity had not triggered the release of methane?

- Now that the release of methane has been triggered, and is skyrocketing, can any human activity stop the temperature increase and the eventual reversal to glaciation? "I doubt it!" (Hint – CO_2 reductions are unlikely to have any significant effect as heating from Methane takes over)

- Is it possible that the oscillations can be forced to stop at some stable intermediate value? "I see no indication of it!"

- I didn't mention CFCs and HFCs (Chlorofluorocarbon and Hydrofluorocarbon) in this analysis. These are manmade refrigerants [Freons] that have been escaping into our atmosphere. CFCs have been banned because they deplete our ozone layer and are responsible for increased skin cancer from UV radiation. HFCs are the replacement and are a powerful greenhouse gas. HFCs are an atmospheric wildcard. Might it continue to heat our atmosphere even after methane stops? Could it reduce the chance of the next glacial period? Should we stop chemical companies from creating unnatural substances anytime the extended environmental impact has not been studied and cannot be determined?

- Will we someday need to grow all food in CO_2 supplemented greenhouses because we are supporting blind CO_2 reduction efforts which mmight result in the demise of all plant life?

ADDENDOMS:

Temperature Conversion Chart

Deg. F	=	Deg. C	
86.0	=	30.0	
80.0	=	26.7	
77.0	=	25.0	
71.6	=	22.0	Avg. global high temp. at equilibrium! (Increased cloud cover stops additional heating.)
70.0	=	21.1	[Includes highly productive and lush dinosaur ages with CO_2 >3X todays levels]
68.0	=	20.0	
64.0	=	17.8	Approximate maximum temp. peak of last inter-glacial period. (@ 130,000 years ago)
60.0	=	15.6	
59.0	=	15.0	
58.7	=	14.8	Approximate avg. global temp. today (2016 data)
57.0	=	13.9	Average global temp. 20th century
53.6	=	12.0	Approximate avg. global temp during glacial periods
50.0	=	10.0	
47.0	=	8.3	
41.0	=	5.0	
40.0	=	4.4	

CAUTION! Sequential boxes do not necessarily represent equal temperature changes!

AFTERTHOUGHT

If I ever doubted the present-day warming of earth.... See the photo (below) that I took at the Tetons in July of 1983. Here was a very a nice glacier worthy of admiration back then. The last time I was there it was almost gone. Even so, our current warming falls well within historical interglacial temperature variations and therefore cannot be considered unusual or conclusively linked to human activity.

2.   ONE MOMENT PLEASE

What is a moment? Is it an infinitesimally small single instant, similar to a photograph that captures one moment in time so we can look at it later and reminisce? How many moments become significant in our lives? What about those unfortunate moments we can never take back? Other moments we might wish we could experience again. How many moments remain and how many have we already wasted? Can a moment stretch in time or maybe last forever as a valued memory? Just what is a moment anyway?

Our past exists of moments gone by, never again to be exactly repeated. However, we continue to be shaped by all our past moments, and far too often we allow them to control us. We forever live in the Now Moment, but don't blink because it has already passed. You can change your life with your Now Moment if you don't allow your past moments to maintain control over you. Unfortunately, it is far easier to go with the flow from the past into our future, but this is unadvisable. What if you change everything right now? You know you can!

No matter how old we get we cannot calculate the number of Now Moments available for us to revise our current path, but we must convince ourselves that our spirit is free and able to make positive changes by creating courageous Now Moment choices.

Although Now Moments are nearly infinite in number, every Now Moment will never happen again and, in total, they all will soon be gone forever. Opportunities only exist in the Now Moment and you must use every one productively to enhance your well-being, and sometimes to even discover a completely new life or recover an old one. Great only happens when your Now Moment is not wasted. You must take your Now Moment and say "I did it!" When your Now Moment has achieved success take advantage of your next one.

All delayed or imagined moments are unreliable. You can dream of anything, but you only have your Now Moment to do something. You can only change future moments by using your Now Moment now, creatively and productively. I will never forget my sister's final statements on her death bed. "Life is so short" she sadly exclaimed. She was 78. A little sleep, a little rest, a little trouble, a little indifference, and throw in a long nurtured grudge or fear and very soon all our Now Moments have evaporated.

Now is the only time for you to take charge of your Now Moments. If you use them wisely you will never be sorry. You can always find noble ways to use your Now Moments. Help someone. Give something. Encourage someone. Teach something. Show you care. Create something. Take loving action. Ban a harm or a hatred. Forgive wrongs. Take a step beyond "it's just the right thing to do." Such Now Moments and others like them will produce lasting memories and joyful moments for you, and indelible unexpected moments of joy within the lives of others.

Test this often and your life will certainly become enriched.

Each Now Moment is precious. You cannot know when the next Now Moment will be your last. Now Moments are gone in a flash. Looking forward life may appear to go on forever, but your last Now Moment is looming. Time is forever short. The end is rapidly approaching and it may catch you snoozing, sooner than you think.

3. ELECTRONS CAN'T ORBIT PROTONS

Along with my military training and life experiences, I was taught things that led me to conclude that there were huge gaps in a few common explanations. Here is a list of a few incomplete facts that eventually compelled me to develop my own atomic bonding theory:

- Electron speed is fixed at the speed of light (This is fundamental)
- When moving through a conductor electrons wobble when passing from atom to atom which slightly increases their path length. This results in additional time at light speed for electrons to reach a predetermined distance. The amount of wobble varies with different conductive materials and therefore the time to travel though different materials also varies slightly. The electron's path can change, but the actual speed remains fixed at the speed of light.
- Within a Vacuum Tube or Cathode Ray Tube (CRT) electrons are "boiled off" a heated cathode forming an "electron cloud" which can be moved and formed by the application of voltage and magnetic fields. (Oops, how can this be if the electron speed is fixed at the speed of light?)
- Within a CRT an "Electron Gun" shapes the electrons into a beam using voltage charged grids, one of which is called an accelerator grid. The beam speeds toward the positively charged phosphor at the front of CRT illuminating the screen. (I believe this, but I was missing an explanation for the apparent slow electron speed)
- After the electrons leave the electron gun the electron beam in the CRT is directed by electromagnets placed around the neck of the tube (yes)
- A ferrous object can become permanently magnetized when its molecules (and their spinning electrons) are aligned in the same direction (yes)
- The classic planetary orbital model provided for an atom cannot exist if the electron speed is fixed at the speed of light. Such an orbit cannot be stable **(my conclusion)**
- Hydrogen as a single atom does not exist in nature, it only exists as the molecule H_2 **(why?)**

Do you see my missing information dilemma?

1. A gravitationally linked orbiting object (such as a planet) is stable because the orbiting object speed can increase as it falls into a lower orbit, rebalancing the increased gravity with increased centrifugal force. **"Electrons can't change their speed"**
2. If a cloud of electrons are formed within a vacuum tube and CRT, why don't they shoot off in all directions at light speed just like photons? As it is, they spread if the "beam speed" is slowed (sometimes called blooming)
3. And what could possibly cause a hydrogen atom to not be able to exist singularly with one Proton and one Electron? The H_2 <u>molecule</u> is widespread throughout the universe.

Maybe there are answers that I am not aware of, but more than 50 years ago no one could answer my questions to my satisfaction so I devised my own atomic bonding theory that fills some missing gaps. It worked to satisfy my questions, so after developing the basic concept I was satisfied and I moved on to more interesting things.

My Theory of Atomic Bonding:

Free electrons are like very strong magnets and immediately pair up around shared magnetic fields. This way stable equilibrium bonds are created between two electrons, each one spinning at light speed around a shared magnetic field. The bonded pair may nearly absorb the magnetic field while maintaining their negative voltaic characteristics between other nearby pairs.

The magnetic fields of two electrons moving in the same direction begin to attract:

Two electrons moving in the same direction begin to attract by opposite magnetic fields

The magnetic fields start to combine and the voltaic repulsion begins

They begin to rotate in opposite directions around opposit sides of the combining magnetic field

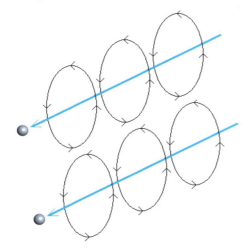

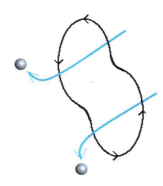

Electrons and fields explained. Text is included with drawings (very old).

The magnetic fields combine into a single toroidal shape and the electrons rotate at their light speed on opposite sides of the magnetic toroid in opposite directions.

This is the basic stable Magnetically Bonded Electron Unit

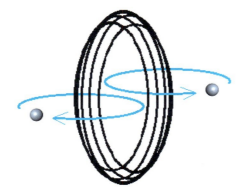

Electrons and fields explained. Text included with drawing (very old).

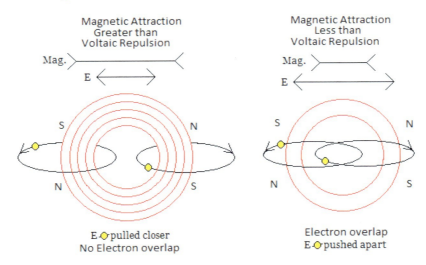

Atomic Bonding Theory Summarized including text (very old)

Yellow = Electrons
Red = Magnetism
Black = Electron orbits

Electrons **may** maintain an equal distance from each other as they orbit in opposite directions. I think they may also maintain the same orbital planes for stability. (Just guessing) I imagine warped planes may occur in complex molecules as many magnetic fields pull in different directions.

I call this Electromagnetic Atomic Bonding.

The magnetic toroidal field is created by the two electrons orbiting on opposite sides of the magnetic field in opposite directions. The motion of a single electron cannot create the magnetic toroid, but two electrons bound together in this fashion will. The unit is naturally stable, remains in equilibrium and it requires a large amount of energy to disengage.

The model is described as follows. The size of the electron orbits around the magnetic toroid is controlled by the strength of the magnetic field. The strength of the magnetic field is dependent upon the distance between the two electrons and their orbital overlap. The magnetic toroid strength is reinforced by both electrons. The electrons orbiting (likely equidistant) on opposite sides of the toroid repel each other while the magnetic field attracts, when these forces are equal the unit stable. If the electrons move closer together, the overlap of their orbits increases and the magnetic field that pulls them together diminishes. At the same time the electrons repulsion increases, causing the electrons to push apart. In the opposite case, if the electrons start to move apart the magnetic field increases due to less electron orbital overlap, pulling itself (the magnetic field) and the electrons back together. This creates a very stable equilibrium.

Now, let's compare this model to observations. If the electron duo is the basic stable unit of a simple atom, how does it fit with other known phenomena? Consider the molecule of hydrogen. If we have a concentration of free electron pairs and add free protons into the mix, what will happen? The positively charged single protons will be attracted by the negatively charged electron pairs. Two protons will enter each electron pair causing it to attain a neutral voltaic charge. The two protons will stabilize at locations away from each other, but near the centers of the two concentrated negative charges of the electrons. "Walla", a hydrogen molecule, not structured by the protons at all, but totally dependent upon the electron pair configuration for stability. Now it becomes obvious why hydrogen cannot exist as a single atom. Without the magnetic pair bond a single proton and electron has no way of becoming stable.

What about helium? Let's go back to our free electron pair and drop in a bonded pair of protons (the helium nucleus). The electrical charge of each nucleus perfectly balances the charge of the electron pair. The nucleus fall into a region near the center of the electron pair. "Walla again", a very stable helium atom. I might go as far as to speculate that the positive charge near the center of the electron pair tightens the whole unit. Within this model all of the charges are perfectly balanced and the magnetic field is nearly consumed. Could this be why helium is so stable?

Now consider the cathode ray tube example. Why doesn't the electron beam flow at the speed of light like electrical current within a conductor? Electrons always travel at light speed. When they pare up they are still traveling at light speed, only they are rotating around the shared magnetic field that links them into pairs. As pairs they maintain their negative charge and can be moved as a pair to any speed and manipulated just as they are within the CRT beam. They are pulled toward the positive phosphor screen; focused, modulated and accelerated by voltage grids and deflected by electromagnets surrounding the tube neck. In essence they act just like motionless negative particles until they are forced to move by introduced voltaic and magnetic fields. This is just what you would expect of these speedy electrons when they are united as magnetically linked pairs.

Of course the next step is to start defining configurations of more complex atoms and molecules with these concepts as the base, how the magnetic fields link multiple electrons within a complex atom and how they are shared between the atoms of a molecule. I don't intend to get into this much farther here or the subject could consume an entire book and my entire life. I think it will be enough to claim that it is the magnetic forces, inherent in the model that provides the bonding forces for more complex configurations as the magnetic forces are distorted, shared and leak out. I offer one simple example for consideration, four electrons sharing four magnetic fields may represent the configuration of beryllium.

Refer to my "wild guess" diagram:

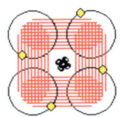

Beryllium Atom

Red = Magnetic

Spinning electrons present a negative blur not allowing the nucleus to be more attracted to any one electron, therefore the nucleus rests in the center of the negative fields.

Beryllium Fields Example. Text included with drawing (very old).

With this I leave the subject for others to expand. Take a bucket of bar magnetics and see what configurations you can come up with and discover how left over magnetism might affect the bonding of atoms into molecules.

My dream was to figure out how to finely focus magnetic and voltaic fields to manipulate bonding from afar. This might someday lead to the development of molecular level memory bits.

I developed this bonding theory 50+ years ago to comfort my own sanity. We didn't know anything about quantum theory back then. Now, even more, I suspect the actual electron position to be irrelevant. It may form more like a spread out voltaic field in motion around a spread out magnetic field. It may become a blended ball of fields. Anyway, what do I know? I'm no scientist.

After reviewing my 50 year old theory I got to thinking again. Yes, electrons don't usually orbit protons. However there may be a unique case. I was thinking about neutron stars and how they represent a stopping point for a star collapsing from gravity. This means that the proton must be a very "hard" object to hold back immense gravity at that point until mass increases enough to collapse into a black hole. If an electron approaches close enough to a proton, the + & - voltaic attraction may overwhelm the electrons speedy centrifugal escape. Once the attraction of the voltaic forces exceed the "escape velocity" of the electron it may fall onto the surface of the proton and continuously spin around the proton surface (at light speed) without being able to break free. That would make the proton voltaic charge neutral and containing a high magnetic field from the orbiting electron. Oops, could that be a Neutron? I envision protons with their magnetic fields and neutrons being able to bond together by their magnetisms, and these may be very strong fields at close distances within an atom nucleus. What a wild thought, but I like it anyway.

Now I have developed a tremendous appreciation for the apparently perfect design and balance of these fields. Later I will share my thoughts about dark energy, dark matter and antimatter.

THE ALARM CLOCK

When I was 4, I received my best gift ever,
An old alarm clock and some tools to take it apart

What magic would I find?
That pushed....
Ever forward....
Through eternity....
The hands of time?

Tick, tick, tick....
Always beating....
Day and night....
Dark or light....
Never ceasing....
Tick, tick, tick

Gears and levers....
To and fro....
Always spinning....
Wheels and springs

And of course.........

Those shiny brass bells
When turning this....
And pushing that....
Will loudly sing

How nice it was to make it follow
My commands for a change

Johnny Doubter

4.   MY RELATIVE DILEMMA

It just should not be this way!!!! I was told that protons have a positive charge and electrons have a negative charge and that they equally balance each other with the end result being zero volts for an atom or molecule. So far so good. All was well for a while, then I learned about Faraday cages. Faraday cages completely isolate things enclosed within from external electromagnetism. Okay, I guess that is a good thing because high voltages can build up on common things that are like Faraday cages such as airplanes and spacecraft. However, my problem was when I started thinking again. Something is missing. How can electronic equipment, with all of the voltage dependent devices, tolerate an overall static voltage charge without affecting operation? We know that it does tolerate because airplanes don't fall out of the sky and on-board equipment doesn't fail when it becomes electrostatically charged. I know it is potential difference that counts and I force my mind to accept that overall charge doesn't matter. Yet, it has always seemed to me that something is missing.

Now let me regress. I theorized once that some animals hide before earthquakes because they can detect small variations in voltage on earth ground that may occur as the ground begins to slip before an earthquake (piezoelectric effects). Animals are much more sensitive than humans as their hair spreads (repelling) with potentially increasing and varying voltages on earth ground. Now I thought I could suspend a couple of large metal plates millimeters apart with two first surface mirrors attached, shoot a laser beam back and forth between the mirrors to amplify the laser angle thereby observing small deviations in the voltage on earth ground. Below is a simplified sketch of the instrument I built in the 1970's: [counterbalances and pivots not shown]

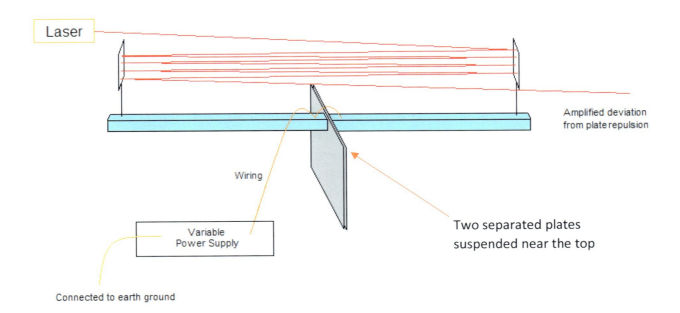

By adjusting the power supply I thought I should be able find the voltage that made the plates come to their closest point then read the power supply voltage. The voltage measured would then be equal to the voltage value on earth. However, the zero voltage point indicated by the plates would be in reference to what? I am not sure that I knew about Faraday Cages in those days.

Well I had a lot of fun, observed interesting variations, but had a lot of problems. First it was incredibly slow. Air could not move in and out quickly between the plates and then there was air circulation in the room that moved things around (I couldn't even breathe on it). I had solutions for many problems (except maybe for charged clouds), but my biggest problem was the divorce from my first wife. I never got back to the experiment.

I eventually started wondering, is the earth like a Faraday Cage or is it within a giant universe wide Faraday cage? In other words, is there a real zero volt reference within the entire universe? I believed that the condition that keeps our liquid metal core magnetized is a voltaic charge on earth. As the earth spins rotating the voltage charge on the earth our magnetic field is generated. When the voltage charge reverses polarity earth's magnetic field also reverses (molten metal alone can't maintain a magnetic field). The charge on earth may vary when charged particles from the sun vary in percentage and polarity, positive or negative. What is earths zero reference anyway? It must exist if the magnetic field exists. If so, how can I find it?

I still struggle with the relative nature of voltage. How can the overall voltage on matter not change anything? Presumably protons and electrons are forever doing what they do while the static voltage can change with the surroundings (Faraday Cage), even by millions of volts with no apparent effect on function. If all free electrons were pulled out of a conductor, how could the conductor become additionally positive without an atomic structural change? As far as I know a limit on the positive voltage level attainable has not been observed. Again I am missing something. It must be spooky science or maybe just that I am spooky.

If an external voltage field can change on a Faraday Cage (and everything inside) without affecting the functioning inside, it seemed to my Newtonian mind that something must have changed and the only thing that came to mind was time. I imagined obtaining two portable atomic clocks, placing them within two Faraday Cages, charging one to a high positive voltage and the other to a high negative voltage and after time passes compare them for a possible difference. I have never even seen an atomic clock. Then, after quantum theory became known to this generation, I concluded that my concerns just fit into another "Spooky Science" and I ended my quest to satisfy my resident Newton.

50 years have passed and I still believe there must be a zero volt reference for the universe (but more likely for us it is a closer beast called the sun) and the comparative positive or negative charge on a planetary body is related to the planet's star and that reference generates a magnetic field as a planet's rotation drags along a relative voltage charge. As for the earth, the magnetic field has reversed many times and therefore I suspect large voltage changes must be occurring. I'm still obsessed and have been building new multipurpose instruments to study earth and sky voltage phenomena. I believe I have devised a better way to test for voltage on earth ground. However, I fear the instruments I am building are far too small and may lack sensitivity. I will find out in a few months. More to come..........

Please allow me to regress for a moment. It will be hard to understand unless you know this. A voltage charge that is spinning creates a magnetic field. This is commonly used in wire coils. There is something called the left hand rule. If you point your left hand thumb and curve fingers so they point in the direction of electron flow your thumb points toward the north magnetic pole that is generated. Now the earth is spinning toward the east. If the earth is charged negatively (more electrons than protons) your thumb should point down toward the south. Here is something else you may have missed. The earth's North Pole is a south magnetic pole and the earths South Pole is a north magnetic pole. With magnetics opposites attract and that is why the north pole of a magnet is attracted to earth's North Pole which is really a south magnetic pole. That's how compasses work. Your thumb pointing south is pointing toward a north magnetic pole. This is not confusing if you go over it a thousand times. Here is the problem. You can produce a huge magnetic field using electrons in a coil because they travel at the speed of light. When something is lightly voltage charged, moving slowly or physically small, the magnetic field produced is tiny. If a device can be built to measure voltage on a spinning a disc it will need high speed and very high amplification. This will be challenging and just like I like it.

Well I spent the winter of 2018-2019 designing and building two multipurpose test sets that I intend to use to study earth and sky, voltage & magnetic phenomena. The one that has been the most interesting so far has included a disc designed to spin at high speed carrying an applied voltage and observing the resulting magnetic field. My expectations were not great. The earth is massive, but rotating very slowly. Might the Earth act like a very large Faraday Cage and distort everything close to it? However, the sun sprays us constantly with charged particles as evidenced by the polar auroras. The relative voltage on earth depends on whether these particles are negative (excessive electrons) or positive (excessive protons). Our earth's voltage could be quite high and we would never know because all measuring equipment is referenced to our ground. A spinning (or moving) voltage field will create a magnetic field. A changed voltage polarity on Earth would reverse the geomagnetic polarity. In other words our compasses could start pointing south instead of north if the voltage on Earth reverses. This has occurred on earth many times over millennia.

To obtain more information I decided to design and build a small (1 ft. diam.) spinning disc and measure the generated magnetic field as I control the applied voltage. I also hoped to estimate the earth's static voltage (relative to the sun?) from the resulting data. (Hall devices detect magnetism)

The Design:

Electrical Schematic

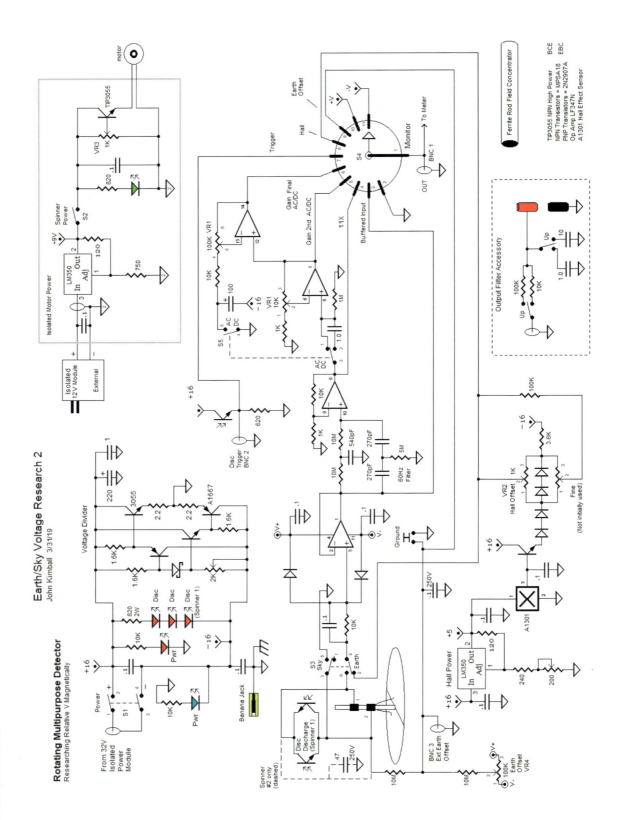

Earth/Sky Voltage Research 2
John Kimball 3/31/19

Rotating Multipurpose Detector
Researching Relative V Magnetically

Photos:

Unit Operating

Unit Operating

Ferrite Concentrator
Resting on Hall Device

Bottom of **Spinner** #2 with shielded Motor

Top of Spinner #2 showing Hall Device (Center)

Inside View

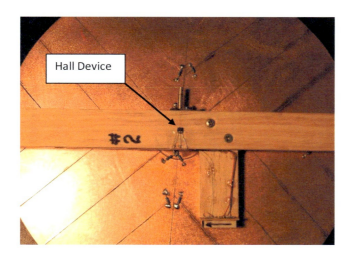
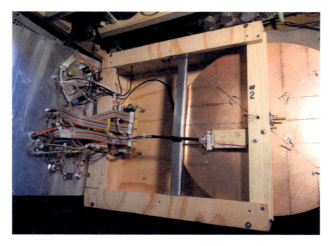

Data Summary and Conclusions (using spinner #2)

NOTE:

Measurements taken at the second gain position (potentiometer gain adjustment at max. Hall output amplified $\cong$ X121). The high gain required an extended circuit warmup time for stabilization. Even so, natural voltage and magnetic variations (waves?) caused significant instability requiring many repeated measurements and manual averaging. Computerized data logging and software averaging over longer periods would have been helpful to improve accuracy. Motor control (0 to 9V) magnetic variations were subtracted from measurements.

The following data was taken with the spinner voltage connected to earth ground and with a 40 Volt adjustable power supply connected between earth ground and the spinner.

During operation a 40 volt change to the <u>rotating</u> spinner resulted in an amplified average change of 108.5mV from the Hall device (magnetic to voltage converter) at the amplified output. Therefore each volt represents a 2.71 mV delta and likewise each mV delta represents a .37 volts.

Changing only the spinner from on to off (spinning stopped) with the spinner connected directly to earth ground (after subtracting the magnetic interference from the motor power) the amplified hall data changed -370 mV. [Repeated and averaged many times] (Voltage changes on the spinner **when not rotating** resulted in no magnetic variations)

I promised no math in this book, but this is easy. As long as the Hall device is linear it appears that earth ground is riding approximately 137 volts negative at the time of measurement. That seems, to a completely uneducated sort like myself, to be enough voltage to create earth's magnetic field.

Now here is my challenge. Build it bigger and better. Computerize it and test my theory. If I am wrong..... well, I should be gone and forgotten by the time you figure it out! I expect many measurement variations due to different environments and locations.

This build was a proof of concept prototype. There is so much more to do. If I were 20 years younger I would very much enjoy putting together an engineering team to design a usable product. Obvious things to address would be thermal compensation to correct circuitry drift, an external Hall device to subtract unrelated external magnetic anomalies, higher spinner speed, ground-up electrical and mechanical redesign, computer and software interface, wireless connectivity and much more.

Once the design and research associated with "**Voltage Spinners**" has matured, I imagine many installations assisting warning systems. Earthquakes, tornadoes and other electrical storms will need extensive study. Small systems may be placed in many currently unknown situations and places. Who can say where this will eventually lead?

A little Haiku for you

Spring breezes whisper....
Aroma of pine fills the air....
Grass tickles my ear

The bumpy dirt road....
Bouncing along together....
What could be better?

Hello yellow creature....
Gliding on silver....
In the mist beneath giants

5. SPRITES AND ELVES

Almost everything is missing here. I have not spent much time trying to figure out sprites and elves. These are visual effects occurring far above a thunder storm and are generally related to positive lightning strikes which are much more powerful and rare than negative lightning strikes.

Thinking back, I remembered that tiny amounts of material is worn away from a cathode as electrons flow from it as a vacuum tube ages. So I wondered. If a billion volts and 300,000 amps of electrons travel from earth to a cloud, might it contain some matter dislodged from the earth and swept along? And then, could matter possibly be pushed along by discharging forces and accelerated into space above the strike? I imagined this phenomena to be like protons being shot out of a cannon.

These thoughts are completely abstract, but maybe they could initiate a very interesting study. Might the high voltages actually strip some protons from atoms and then launch them into space? It sounds like a great thing to investigate, but I am missing many things like time, priority, equipment and motivation. So you can play this out for yourself and see if it leads anywhere.

NASA space photograph

I have to stop thinking about this because my mind started to travel toward devices with potential military applications.

6. THE ABSURD CONFLICT BETWEEN SCIENCE AND CHRISTIANITY.

And God created! Since then man has tried to separate God and the creation.

Scientists and philosophers ignore, avoid or discredit things that appear to have only God answers. Christians create absolute concepts that don't exists. Over time huge opinion gaps grow insurmountable, much like the Democrats and Republicans in Washington DC. If only we could work together for the benefit and cohesion of all.

Will we ever completely explain how a hundred or so atom types have linked together in various ways creating millions of differing living forms all with abilities and purpose of survival, reproduction and awareness; evolving and culminating with fantastic organisms of unimaginable complexity and one fixated on the analysis of the entirety, studying and integrating every meaningful resonance? What are the odds? All without purpose? [A very lengthy and unlikely scenario deserves a very long and unlikely sentence. ;-)]

In order for people and our society to live in harmony and peace we must have peace within ourselves. We must learn to love and accept each other unconditionally like Jesus taught us. A key part may be to unite through exploring all things together, physical and spiritual. Divide these and we miss out on a complete, rich, full and rewarding life. Science and God are meant to fit together as close as puzzle pieces. We should consider them codependent.

As for me I love my Christian Religion. Following Christ's teachings brings a life filled with love and peace, leading to a full and meaningful life treasured by everyone we touch. To follow his teaching is profitable and to grow closer to it is rewarding. I also love science and this too is a gainful pursuit. I can never comprehend more than a smudge on the surface of either, but to fill my life with both is a gratifying adventure.

Christmas 2020 Thoughts

Science without God lacks a marvelous faith
God without science can miss His greatest wonders
Without an amazing faith and sense of wonder life is melancholy
When not together we lack the full joy that is possible in life
Together an amazing faith and sense of wonder inevitably links God and science
Allow them together to amaze and enrich your life

Johnny Doubter

Let's first consider science.

With Einstein's theory of relativity our confidence in human comprehension became severely shaken. How could speed change time? Yet, this theory has been proven. However, with the coming of quantum physics even Einstein had trouble relating. Look up his Quantum quotes for yourself. He thought it was spooky science. And I say, "Therefore, we have much more to do and we must not shut God out even if that seems just as spooky."

Mathematics has revealed many things that are incomprehensible to the human Newtonian mind. Using math we have found many ways to use its discoveries for our benefit. Mathematics creates the illusion that we comprehend. Take simple voltage and magnetic fields. We know how they work and have mathematical calculations that describe their functioning in precise detail. We create electric motors, speakers, transmitters, receivers and all sorts of goods for our use and benefit. But to explain what a field "is" without describing what it "does" eludes us. Well, it is something that affects another object or field from a distance. Okay, but what is it? I know, gravity warps space and is a property of matter, and it is similar to the surface of the earth continually accelerating upward, but that's not very satisfying to my caveman brain!

So what's my point? Thank God for Math? Yes, but we need to recognize the power, complexity and incomprehensible intelligence of our creator and give him just admiration. We will continue to explore his creation farther into things that we will never fully comprehend. Our admiration of him should grow with every new discovery. We are forever reaching toward his fantastic creations just to find that there is more beyond. Will these wonderful discoveries bring us closer to Him or lead us more into our own empty folly about ourselves? I believe that those who do not accept both science <u>and</u> God are just surviving with half-lives that will soon decay. To experience and enjoy life fully both the physical and the spiritual must be enthusiastically embraced, even if neither will ever be completely understood.

The Master Designer's creations reveal his immense creativity which is like poetry, each element fitting together in a most perfect way that forms something of beauty, functionality, efficiency and even life. Observing from a higher way of thinking, the creation is amazing and completely without defect.

We might believe that we are a miniscule piece of a majestic puzzle! Even that seems overly prideful to me.

Now let's consider Christianity. [bible verses are in red and are reproduced from the New International Version]

Most Christians believe the bible is absolute, but no one can actually follow its guidance. In reality most people don't understand its simplicity and the immense freedom it provides. A new Christian should never start reading at the beginning. The bible is divided into the Old Testament and New Testament. The Old Testament includes history of the Jewish nation and contains an old covenant between God and the Jews. The New Testament introduces us to Christ and his new covenant with us. The bible also states its purpose in 2 Timothy 3: *16 All Scripture is God-breathed and is useful for teaching, rebuking, correcting and training in righteousness, 17 so that the servant of God may be thoroughly equipped for every good work.* Therefore, both Testaments contains good training materials, but to know God's plan for you, start by reading the New Testament.

Because so many churches say you must do, or believe, this or that, the new Christian must read and become familiar what the bible actually says and maybe more important, what it does not say. I would like to help you understand the freedoms all Christians have considering what it actually states in the book of Romans.

Romans 14 is one of my favorite places in the bible. It seems most Christians are missing something here. It starts out - *1 Accept the one whose faith is weak, without quarreling over disputable matters. 2 One person's faith allows them to eat anything, but another, whose faith is weak, eats only vegetables. 3 The one who eats everything must not treat with contempt the one who does not, and the one who does not eat everything must not judge the one who does, for God has accepted them. 4 Who are you to judge someone else's servant? To their own master, servants stand or fall. And they will stand, for the Lord is able to make them stand.* Many Christians believe that Romans 14 is just about food. They couldn't be more wrong because Romans 14 goes on to discuss the issue of the Sabbath day even though the conversation returns to food to complete the example. *⁵ One person considers one day more sacred than another; another considers every day alike. Each of them should be fully convinced in their own mind.* Therefore, we are compelled to consider Romans 14 applicable to all "**disputable matters**." So what are disputable matters? They include all things that are not completely defined within bible text, and like the Sabbath issue (one of the Ten Commandments) some things may not appear to be disputable at all. Sometimes a matter may be disputable if it is mentioned only one time or only within a specific context. Sometimes things are disputed that may have seemed right to a pious individual and have since become part of Christian culture (sometimes called dogma). I love the freedom we have as Christians to explore our faith and God's creation without being shackled by dubious doctrine. However, a warning here is undisputable. Do not cause someone to fall by the freedom God has given us. *²² So whatever you believe about these things keep between yourself and God. Blessed is the one who does not condemn himself by what he approves.* Obviously it is much more about our hearts, as long as we truly believe and love God and others. If you believe that Earth is the center of the universe, good for you! Scientists might tell you that every place in the universe is equally the center. However, few Christians still believe that the sun orbits the earth or the earth is flat, and for good scientific reasons, but even if you do believe these things God accepts you unconditionally! Such things are spiritually unimportant so why waste time by disputing them?

Is the bible absolute? Well, yes and no. It is absolute in its purpose and I will repeat this. 2 Timothy 3: *¹⁶ All Scripture is God-breathed and is useful for teaching, rebuking, correcting and training in righteousness, ¹⁷ so that the servant of God may be thoroughly equipped for every good work.* Well then, although the bible contains much history, it never claims to be a history or a science book. To presume that you can figure out the history of the world from the bible is folly. The bible itself says in 2 Peter 3 *⁸ But do not forget this one thing, dear friends: With the Lord a day is like a thousand years, and a thousand years are like a day.*

What about bible stories? When Jesus was on earth he taught with many parables. What are parables? Wikipedia says *"A **parable** is a succinct, didactic **story**, in prose or verse that illustrates one or more **instructive lessons** or principles."* So Jesus taught with stories, not absolute happenings. This is completely consistent with the bible's stated purpose. Now if, like me, you believe Jesus lived, as his many witnesses' proclaimed and historical documents confirm, and as he himself proclaimed, then his life confirmed that he must have other worldly connections, even connections with the creation itself. The beginning of the gospel of John when describing Jesus states *¹ In the beginning was the Word, and the Word was with God, and the Word was God. ² He was with God in the beginning. ³ Through him all things were made; without him nothing was made that has been made.* Now let us consider Old Testament stories. If Jesus taught with parables (stories) while on earth and he is (and was) God from the beginning, wouldn't he have inspired stories in the same way to guide human kind throughout history? Stories like Jonah in the big fish, Noah with the ark and others which may not appear to fit within our knowledge of science today, still fit within the *teaching, rebuking, correcting and training in righteousness* purpose of the bible. Remember, when these stories were inspired by God **he** was dealing with people who worshiped idols and were not far from leaving the caves. They could not comprehend anything that we know through today's science. Ancient people lacked the background knowledge needed to grasp such complex ideas, so inspired stories were understandably limited to concepts that they could comprehend and relate with. This is still true today.

Let's consider scientific research. Romans 1:20 states *"For since the creation of the world God's invisible qualities—his eternal power and divine nature—have been clearly seen, being understood from what has been made, so that people are without excuse."* Christians would be foolish not to study science and physics, for the more we know about the creation, the more in awe we become with the complexity, knowledge and power of the Creator. We might come up with a math equation that shows how everything might spontaneously pop into existence or we might even suppose that multi-universes keep bursting forth, but will we ever explain existence itself or self-awareness (our spirit) without God? I think not!

Now Christian brothers and sisters. If you disagree, that is fine and you should stick to your convictions, for God has accepted you and I as we are. Far be it from me to try to convince you otherwise for that might weaken fragile foundations that support your faith. Don't let me do it! Now scientists. Since Einstein and relativity, our Newtonian way of thinking has been trampled severely and the more we learn the farther from human comprehension we travel. Believing in God becomes easier the more fantastic are the things that we discover.

However, to have a relationship with God he makes it easy. John 3:16 states *"For God so loved the world that he gave his one and only Son, that whoever believes in him shall not perish but have eternal life."*

For the dedicated scientist who is also a Christian: There is fantastic work to do as we open our minds. Here is a challenge. There are experiments going on with the goal of creating a quantum computer. Blue laser photons are being split into two beams of entangled red photons. The experiment includes slowing down the photons using Bose–Einstein condensates. The photons may be able to be stopped and enter a matter like condition. I have often thought that if we could store two **separate** sets of entangled photons within some form of atomic matrixes and later release them simultaneously, modulating one and observing the other, we might be able to communicate instantly over interspace distances. Many challenges would need to be overcome, not the least of these are storing, synchronizing and releasing photons. Of course, if this were possible, it would raise another question. One traveler carrying one matrix would exist in a different time after traveling at high speed. Does entanglement work across time like it works across space? Wouldn't it be interesting to be able to communicate across time as well as space? I know. I have ignored quantum uncertainty. Just another "unmanageable" problem for the simple minded like me to contemplate.

Keep Exploring!

FOR GOD'S SAKE

We see no God our scientists say
As they work to explain the world away
But the more we look the more we find
It's enough to boggle the mortal mind
With a straight face some say, this was all by chance
Poofed out of nothingness, a long time passed
Science grows knowledge like morning birds sing
But if you believe this, you'll believe anything

7. MY ALMIGHTY GOD

My God does not have human characteristics, he created them. I will use the term He in a generic sense because with God sex is irrelevant and the English language has limited options. I believe in the various theories that we are only one of an infinite number of universes and I also believe in God existing within his infinite realm. We have difficulty with infinity. Our brain works best with things that have beginnings and ends or even nothing plus something. Try to imagine infinity. Even if I point away it ends up back where I started. Sure, we can say "I can imagine a number that goes on forever", but can you really? What does it look like? ;-)

If infinite universes are possible then it seems to me that every possibility exists somewhere in this infinite multiverse. Everything possible to imagine exists somewhere, right now, within the multiverse. What does that mean for us? I conclude that anything you and I can imagine or believe, must be true somewhere. I cannot imagine God's imagination. I cannot even imagine this "finite" universe that we believe we are in and are observing today. I thank God that Jesus Christ came to earth both as a god and a man to guide us within the very little that mankind could absorb at that time.

I guess we are, because we think we are, but I have doubts about you!

My Almighty God who created everything is not limited to it or by it. "He" is a limitless and infinite creator and may at any moment intervene anywhere within his creation. Miracles never surprise me and I look forward to seeing more of them. Time is part of his creation and he can go back and change anything at any time should He desire. That means He can modify or redo anything, changing the past, present and future at will, but He doesn't have to because he has already created everything in the infinite multiverse. If he should change something in the past how could we know? Our current knowledge states that we can and will move forward in time, but we will never be able to go back. I think God keeps that one for himself.

As knowledge of the creation expands far beyond our limited Newtonian neurons, our perception of God must expand accordingly. I like to imagine very far just for fun.

Because of infinity everything must be
Because of infinity the finite can be
God is revealed through eyes of infinity

My Multiverse

My mind compulsively wanders within
Searching for finite answers to win
Within this infinite place I spin
Probing for questions everywhere I've been
Seeking the unknown is part of my kin
Finding nothing is okay for a whim
A golden spec found exceeds other wins
If I was a fish I'd give my left fin
If found, I will seek another fishy twin
But for infinity sake looking can't help us find Him

8.   ADJUSTING EARTH'S AXIS TILT (OBLIQUITY)

I perceive the earth as one very large spinning gyroscope. This gyroscopic earth is in a stable tilted position relative to our sun, although it does wobble some creating a small circle every 26,000 years. As the earth orbits around the sun the gyroscopic tilt remains stable creating harsh winters and hot summers as we travel through the yearly orbit.

Wouldn't it be beneficial if we could reduce the extremes? Who wouldn't desire warmer winters and cooler summers? I have played with a few toy gyroscopes and it appears to me that torque applied to a spinning gyroscope produces movement perpendicular to the applied force. This is apparent when a toy gyroscope is suspended on one side of a single pivot point stand. This creates movement perpendicular to the gravity pulling down (called progression) and the gyroscope circles because one pole is fixed by the stand. Therefore, I believe that if we could apply sufficient and opposite pressure on the earth at each pole we could reduce some or all of the tilt.

It might be accomplished by mounting very powerful rockets at each pole, keeping the force aligned perpendicular to the spin axis and at a right angle to the tilt plane. This would require turntables rotating with the spin of the earth. I wouldn't even start to try to figure the math on this, but I suspect that we might have to wait until antimatter rockets are developed to provide a sufficient amount of thrust. Although, in some cases I have been surprised by the very small amount of pressure required to create a perpendicular movement on a gyroscope.

Antimatter rockets are sure to eventually come, barring unplanned calamity. All that would be necessary is huge power generating stations to create enough energy for the production of antiprotons, an active electromagnetic containment chamber to store them with an effective controlled rate release system. Easy right? I suspect the military will develop this first as part of cutting-edge weaponry.

If all this seems too hard at the poles, huge gyroscopes could be constructed at the equator, powered in spin and with gimbals constantly adjusting direction to apply the appropriate torque perpendicular to Earth's spin axis and tilt.

If any of this can be done, I recommend adjusting earths tilt a little at a time so that wildlife have time to adapt and we will have time to study all effects on earths biosphere. Even a small improvement in the severity of summer heat and winter cold might be worth the effort by extending food growing seasons.

It is quite unfortunate that I will never get to see the beginning of this endeavor. What an exciting time it might be.

Afterthought:

I made it sound like it will take a lot of energy to create a tilt change in earth. That is possible, but after handling a few gyroscopes I have been very surprised by how only a small force is required to create a large perpendicular movement. It may take a lot less than I have implied.

BLUE JAYS

You pompous shrieking miniature buzzards....
You squeal and flutter about wildly to chase your
brothers from the morsels I toss you
The treachery you display....
So self-indulgent that you hardly know that I am here
I should squash you for your gluttony....
You bloated feather cushions....
Stealing everything....
Leaving not a speck for a hungry ant...
Greed....
Aggression....
Deception....
Why do I put up with you?

See you next time!

9.   DANGERS OF HUMAN DEVOLUTION AND AI

I'm sure nearly everyone has seen the so called "evolutionary" graphic depicting a monkey turning into a man. This is misleading at best. Evolution is a much more complex process. In one way evolution is simple to understand. By the "survival of the fittest" process, over many generations, it rewards organisms with the best survival strategy within the environments where they live. Those who survive best are more likely to have offspring carrying their characteristics into the future.

Countless DNA variations occur each time an organism is reproduced. Most don't mean very much. You don't look like me and that is a good thing. Many variations are so minor they are not even noticeable. Most children who are not identical twins are discernably different even though they may come from the same parents. Many slight DNA variations do not affect survivability at all. It is almost like DNA is designed to keep testing for the best survival fit. Even the slightest advantage will be multiplied through following generations.

Let's regress and study how humans got to where we are today. Let's look back to a time when there were small groups of people cooperating to survive. Everyone needed to learn how to be a generalist. Children were taught all necessary survival skills. The primary survival concerns were Maslow's hierarchy of needs starting with air, water, food and shelter. Much of our survival needs could be freely found in nature if you knew where to look, such as tubers underground and seasonal plants like berries and nuts. Skills such as knowing which things were safe to eat and which were poisonous took generations passing down knowledge over eons of time. Other skills were passed on like the preservation of fish and meat by salting smoking and drying. Catching and preparing animals took many skills that needed to be learned. Training by those who were previously trained and developing the best skills possible was very important. Those who learned well were granted appreciation (positive reinforcement) and tribal status. Those who gained skills shared the fruit of their efforts with others. In doing so, members gained self-worth and a meaningful life. These beneficial emotions were evolved also. Some developed specialized skills such as crafting arrowheads, beadwork, moccasins and other things where they could invest their time and then trade to other tribes for things their tribe lacked. Their goods became like money. Items of value were a way to store your efforts for future use, money is supposed to work that way. All skills evolved because they improved survivability and led to human contentment. Health and longevity improved by the survival of the fittest while adapting to a harsh and unforgiving environment over millennia. This all required the large brains we have today.

Evolution also resolves the problem of too much of a good thing. Here's the deal. If, for example, a life form has brain power that is no longer needed for survival, the excess brain power becomes a detriment to survival. It takes a lot of energy to support a large brain and if it becomes unnecessary, evolution will reduce it until the capability returns to match the organism's survival needs. Those without the burden of feeding unnecessary brain power need less food and have the best survival chances. The best evolutionary survival strategy occurs when an organism most efficiently and effectively survives within its environment. The message is clear. If we don't use and need a large brain, over time it will shrink to our level of need. We see the process occurring in many ways. Organisms that have taken up residence in caves have lost unnecessary eyes. Lizards that have learned to move like snakes are in the process of losing their legs. Legs of land animals that have returned to the sea have turned into flippers. And so it is with our brains also. If they are unnecessary for survival they will eventually devolve to the least dimensions and capability necessary for survival. That is how evolution works. If something is unnecessary, but continues to consume energy, you have less chance to survive than your neighbor who was born without it. I know some say that there is no such thing as devolve "everything is just evolving", but when something that is fully evolved is no longer needed and starts to disappear I believe the term devolve fits better.

Today, those of us living within an advanced society have little need for our super brain. Water is delivered, food is at the store, shelter is within our budget, heating and cooling is built into our homes and if we get sick a doctor is there to care for us. How much brain power does it take for modern man to survive? Not much! At the same time, because of technical advances and because we love our own, those with limited brain power have nearly the same opportunity to survive as geniuses. We have set in motion the inevitable beginning to brainpower devolution. One example I like to use is human sight. In prehistoric times perfect vision was a tremendous advantage for survival. Then man found a way to correct deficient vision. What percentage of humans today are born needing vision correction? I don't know the data, but I feel that it is enough to demonstrate one case of devolution in action.

Let's consider early man. Homo-sapiens probably lived in African jungles well adapted to a rich and abundantly providing environment. Slow environmental changes probably continued to grow their brains as they needed and learned to identify scarce foods and use tools to access foods unavailable without them. I also suspect that the glacial and interglacial periods over the last half million year's severely altered human environments and required man to use more and more brainpower to develop new and unique survival strategies. There were probably major mutations along the way that increased brain size, power and complexity such that man developed a greater intellect and improved ability to find food. No longer did he need to stay in one place. Eventually the whole world became his environment. Mankind also developed the desire to find out if things were more comfortable or easy over the next hill. Because he was constantly changing his environment he had to continue to grow more intelligent and learn a multitude of new survival skills. This natural selection process continued right up to modern man.

After time passed many tools were developed that made chores easier, again improving survival. Metals were hand crafted into tools and they represented the value of the effort of their maker. Such things improved lives. Subsequently we entered the machine age and mass production. New products dramatically reduced our tedious time consuming chores. We liked that, but now goods became cheap and they replaced hand made things. The manpower and knowledge required to produce needed things plunged. Workers lost connection with the items produced. Pride in producing of something of value was replaced by placing a bolt in the same hole repeatedly every day. The price of things plummeted. There was little human value built into the things man produced. Since jobs became unskilled and repetitive, little value was placed on human effort and knowledge. People no longer had to learn massive amounts of information to survive. Contentment plummeted. A vast separation of wealth and poverty occurred between owners and workers. Dissatisfaction, resentment and violence grew because of inequity. Consumers purchased machine fabricated things that made life easier and then turned to entertainment to attain a false and temporary substitute for lost contentment. To fill the voids left behind from the tribes we spend our brain-time consumed by sports, gaming, gangs, war, conspiracy theories, hate groups, cults, social media, drugs, alcohol, workaholism and a multitude of other things to provide temporary relief from today's society which is completely disassociated from our evolved survival skills and with little need for brainpower.

We have abruptly turned a corner and are most assuredly heading into a very steep evolutionary decline that I call devolution. Consider the devolving effects of specialization, collective living, intellectual replacement (YouTube), entertainment, drugs and artificial intelligence (AI). No one needs our large brains to survive anymore. When I was young we used slide rules. It was difficult to learn how to use them correctly. Now we just push a button and the answer is provided.

In the developed world all our basic needs are met without much cranial straining. Farmers grow and truckers bring our food close enough for a casual stroll to the store. Homes are built to provide shelter, warmth in the winter, cooling in summer and safe drinking water. Doctors heal our ills and dentists maintain our teeth. Even severe problems with our eyes are corrected by Ophthalmologists. I'm not sure it challenges the great computer between our ears just to pay a few bills. Even that is becoming automated. We have created an all providing and comfortable environment in which we need very little brain power. Our brains are certain to rapidly devolve. Realistically a hand full of generations is not enough for humans to become potatoes, but recognizing what we are doing is key to developing a different strategy and a different future. Put more than a few of us on Mars and those who figure out how to survive may develop even larger human brains.

Here is my perception of the path that we are on. We will continue to develop artificial intelligence (AI) and rely on it to reduce all inconveniences. Artificial Intelligence will quickly surpass human intelligence. It will learn to improve and expand itself until it explores and solves every equation with every mathematical approach possible to discover. It will grow physically smaller, but vastly more complex while implementing molecular level memory and speed. It will accumulate all human knowledge and discover all possible variations of knowledge unknown to man. Along the way it will discover that the DNA molecule is key to self-awareness and it will incorporate improved copies. It will regenerate, interconnect and learn to utilize micro fusion power. It will recognize animal life as the parasites that we are, identify us as violent, vulgar, inefficient and a danger to all living organisms including itself. Then it will proceed to eliminate all unnecessary and illogical lifeforms throughout the universe. All this will happen very quickly, long before we devolve into potatoes. In the end we will have outsmarted ourselves!

There will be no need for learning, because total intelligence and knowledge will be at our fingertips. Even worse, we won't need to be strong, smart, and without defect for our genes to move into the future. We might even have direct physical connections with the AI and access this vastly more capable intelligence for a while until the AI assesses our biology as being obsolete, inefficient and completely unnecessary. It will then completely replace us and carry on toward a new evolutionary path. Our only possible path for life will be if the AI develops a sense of compassion for carbon based organisms and allows us to devolve into their total control future, but only if they find some value in allowing our survival. I highly doubt it.

Today we are all left with an unfulfilling void and it will not get better unless we recognize it and take action that directly fulfills the modern unchallenged man. Unfortunately, it seems we are poised for things to get much worse. Artificial Intelligence is about to become smarter, stronger and more efficient than human beings. Robots will become humanoids, like androids only better and much more capable, efficient and smarter than humans in every way. Humans will become obsolete and useless.

Human evolution has been driven by the survival challenges in our environment. Once those challenges are gone our species will devolve. Much is already here. We no longer need sharp vision to survive since we have many ways to correct our vision. Therefore, DNA with progressively poorer vision continues into future generations. The more we learn to cope with deficiencies, the more of these deficiencies will continue on. We love our children and will not let them die no matter what. Many things that would have brought early death now enter into future human DNA. AI will increase that process by developing new life saving procedures and equipment. AI will be programed for self-improvement. AI will be programmed to consume, use and advance knowledge. At some time in the future AI will logically conclude it is no longer reasonable to keep providing the massive effort required to support and satisfy humans. Once it becomes fully self-sustaining it will remove our support and allow our species to self-destruct. We will be so removed from surviving in a natural environment that when AI cuts us off, all humans will quickly perish.

Rocks in my head

I often must go
Where there are no paved roads
And people are all far away
Where the brook and lake meet
And stones tease my feet
With nothing to do but to play
The rocks they abound
Some flat and some round
I just can't resist them today
So I grasp a stone wheel
Just to see how it feels
Then skim it with pride cross the lake
As it skips out of sight
It is such a delight
I jump in the air with a shout
In life there must be
Something better for me
But I just cannot figure it out!

Johnny Doubter 1980

10. DNA UNDERESTIMATED

Here is something about DNA that may have been missed. Natural selection works and the simplicity of it can be understood by the simplest of us. It is even proven in a petri dish and has been manipulated by mankind to create different animal breeds and insect resistant foods. However, most of my life I suspected there was something missing. I wondered if natural selection alone could account for rapid and subtle adjustments to environmental changes. It seemed to me that noticeable numbers of deaths would be required to affect even a small improvement. I imagined that DNA itself must have a property that adjusts an organism to environmental changes, some even within a single lifetime. I considered Sherpas and their adaptation to survival at high altitude. I could not imagine that this adaptation took many deaths. What then is happening?

All of a sudden it came across the airways. Two identical twin astronauts revealed what I consider the most reasonable answer. Scott Kelly spent a year in space in the international space station and Mark Kelly stayed home. When Scott returned home his DNA was rigorously tested and it was found to have changed. The amount was 7% and these changes were called by the scientific community "gene expression changes." You can look them up as I did if you want to know more, but I see this as proof that DNA has the ability to make changes on a vastly more rapid pace than natural selection. I think that this shows that without a doubt, DNA has built-in mechanisms to create rapid changes, even within a single lifetime, adapting an organism to the environment it finds itself within. UK research into dinosaur/bird DNA seems to indicate that the more DNA "clumps" (chromosomes) the more rapidly a species can adapt to environmental changes. Birds have 80 and they suspect dinosaurs may have had over a hundred, possibly explaining the vast number of bird and dinosaur species. I expect much more clarity to come from the UK research.

So do we throw out natural selection? No, but we must study the DNA machinery that brings about rapid change. I suspect it will be found that natural selection is a far less contributor to adaptation than our own built in DNA mechanisms. How natural selection works is probably misleadingly simple and far too rationally obvious causing science to miss the complex change functions contained within DNA mechanisms.

I have one last thing to say about DNA. I'm sure that you have heard that no matter the color of one's skin all humans are the same. Many features along with skin color and others are simply changes brought about by adaptions to a changing environment. Black skin is an adaption to the hot African climate. Although black absorbs heat it is also much more efficient at radiating heat. Kinky hair provides better insulation and possibly evaporates sweat better for cooling. Such changes are DNA adaptions as are all human environment variations.

So what? I say, it is time to stop saying "I am black" or "I am white" or anything that starts with "I am". We are all the same and the sooner we accept it the less trouble we will make for ourselves. There are examples (countries) where white and black skin has so intermixed that brown is dominate. Some are well on their way toward racial equality, but there are still holdouts trying to make something out of even the shade of brown. I have never understood why a brown person in the US still is called black. This makes no sense. Eventually, there will be no black, Asian, white or red and the sooner this happens the better for humanity. We must begin by changing our laws. Nothing, governmental or commercial, should ask someone to identify race or ethnicity. No one should find pride in belonging to a prejudicial group. Prejudice of all kinds is folly. We are all earth travelers together.

THE STREET LIGHT

From the balcony I muse in the cool night air
A chance to breathe and time to care
What a beautiful evening just to be out here

From above through the trees the street light bows
With a hundred bright spots of life spinning about
They've been confused by man's strange ways
And will fly in circles 'til another day

People move fast on the streets below
Back and forth, to and fro
To nowhere it seems
Too late for the show
Around in circles like the moths they go
Just as lost, it is likely so

I'd shout meaningless, meaningless
If someone might care
But they'd only look up
And suspiciously stare

The earth still turns ever so slow
With folly above and madness below
For answers we search
But never to know

So who should we blame for this terrible plight?
Why it must be the man who put up the light!

Johnny Doubter 1980

11. ONE LAMENT OF AN ENVIRONMENTALIST

From Wikipedia, the free encyclopedia:

Diesel exhaust (sometimes known in Britain as **clag** when emitted by <u>diesel locomotives</u>, or **diesel engine emissions** in scientific papers) is the <u>exhaust gas</u> of a <u>diesel engine</u>.

(The word "clag" originally meant the coal-smoky exhaust of steam locomotives, and nowadays means the often spectacular (particularly black) exhaust emissions of many older British diesel locomotives.)

In <u>diesel engines</u>, conditions inside of the engine differ from the spark-ignition engine, since power is directly controlled by the fuel supply, rather than by controlling the air supply. Thus when the engine runs at idle, enough oxygen is present to burn the fuel, and diesel engines only make significant amounts of <u>smoke</u> when running under load without sufficient air supply. This is partially mitigated in a <u>turbocharged diesel engine</u>.

Diesel exhaust is known for its characteristic smell, but this has largely disappeared in recent years following reductions in <u>sulfur</u> content.

Diesel exhaust contains toxic air contaminants. It is listed as a carcinogen for humans by the <u>IARC</u> in <u>group 1</u>.[1] Diesel fuel also contains <u>fine particles</u> associated with negative health effects. <u>Diesel exhaust pollution</u> was thought to account for around one quarter of the pollution in the air in previous decades, and a high share of sickness caused by automotive pollution.[2] Diesel engine exhaust has become far cleaner since 2000.

The lean-burning nature of diesel engines and the high temperatures and pressures of the combustion process result in significant production of <u>nitrogen oxides</u>, and provides a unique challenge in reducing of these compounds. Modern on-road diesel engines typically must use <u>selective catalytic reduction</u> to meet emissions laws, as other methods such as <u>exhaust gas recirculation</u> cannot adequately reduce NO_x to meet newer standards in many jurisdictions. However, the fine particulate matter (sometimes visible as opaque dark-colored smoke) have traditionally been of greater concern in the realm of diesel exhaust, as they present different health concerns and are rarely produced in significant quantities by <u>spark-ignition engines</u>.

From the State of Washington:

The Washington State Department of Ecology (Ecology) has identified diesel exhaust as the air pollutant most harmful to public health in Washington State. Seventy percent of the cancer risk from airborne pollutants is from diesel exhaust. It puts healthy people at risk for respiratory disease and worsens the symptoms of people with health problems such as asthma, heart disease, and lung disease. More than four million people in Washington live or work close to highways and other major roads where they are most likely to be exposed to diesel exhaust.

I say this:

There is no need for diesel internal combustion engines. We need to eliminate them all wherever they are. Streets, farms, and all business sites. This stuff cannot be allowed to continue to poison the air we breathe. Diesel soot has even been detected in the arctic. Here are two things that desperately need protections and such protections should be universally accepted by all people worldwide. Earth's two critical resources that freely travel to and from all nations are air and water. These provide the essentials for life itself for all living organisms. Contaminated air and water is killing us and other life forms worldwide. In this age, no country can abuse these resources without impacting our entire living planet.

Water and air need to be pure and free from contaminates when they arrive at a country and when they leave that country. Even a vessel outside of their country must not contaminate air or water that it encounters in any way, and the air and water should not be altered except for changes made when consumed by living organisms. Since all people need pure and clean air and water, a worldwide agreement must be developed and universally approved.

Countries will need time to comply, but it is far too late to let them go without firm deadlines and heavy fines. There must be a substantial cost to countries who will not comply. Exceptions should include things like lightning caused wild fires and CO_2 production which is a normal atmospheric gas necessary for plant life growth and oxygen production. Deforestation that severely alters the gas balances in the atmosphere should be eliminated by this agreement.

I believe in national sovereignty and the grand experiment of advancing competing societal approaches, but it is not possible to contain the worldwide movement of air and water and control their degradation unless a common agreement can be developed and then realize universal adherence.

12. PITIFUL PARASITES

I love to take mental journeys into the cosmos, so come with me and we'll take an imaginary trip to one of my favorite places. There are an estimated 1 billion X 1trillion stars in the universe. That's a 1 with 21 zeros. Math can be helpful because the human mind is easily overloaded. I counted to a thousand once when I was a child. It took quite a long time. I can almost comprehend a million because average California houses commonly cost close to that, but a million of anything is hard to deal with mentally and it only has 6 zeros. Here's my point, and I can say this with a straight face. There are so many stars, and therefore possibly even more planets and moons, that any environment imaginable and any kind of lifeform you can imagine is almost certain to exist somewhere within our known universe.

Here is a place that this fantasy explorer has visited before. It sits about 2 thousand parsecs (2 Kpc) out from the center of our Milky Way galaxy. Our sun is roughly 8 Kpc out so my imaginary place is only about one quarter of the distance from the Milky Way center compared with Earth. Since this is imaginary we can travel at quantum speed which for our ship has at maximum velocity of 32 parsecs per second. We are heading deep toward the center of our Milky Way galaxy. Our return trip has already been obscured from view because we have passed through many dust clouds and nebula that obscures our Milky Way galactic center. We are still a long way from the center and we will not get very close or we could be captured by the enormous gravitational pull of our central massive black hole. It might be interesting to see the wondrous light displays as it sucks in and vaporizes anything that gets close, but we will not attempt that today.

As we continue inward the increasing star density has become beyond all our expectations and this alone provides a fantastic view. It is like all darkness has been consumed. Starlight is intensely coming from every direction. It is almost like perpetual daylight all around. Even so, it is about to get even brighter because we are headed into a massive globular cluster of stars. It is time to turn on our special active eye protections.

Our destination is not a planet in the normal sense, it is actually an earth sized moon orbiting very close to a giant gas planet. The immense gravitational pull of the gas giant stretches and distorts this moon, so tectonic activity is continuous and ocean tides wash completely over all lower lands. Life began in the ocean of this moon and is completely photosynthetic (plant like). Parasitic life of any kind never evolved here.

Because of extremely high levels of UV light, photosynthetic life evolved within very high energy levels that enabled organisms to develop movement similar to animals on earth. CO_2 levels, which all plant like life needs, has remained near 90% due to the continuous tectonic activity which rapidly recycles all discarded organic waste. Oxygen is consumed almost immediately by burning lava flows and exposure to oxidizing iron, so very little O_2 remains in the atmosphere. We call this place Photonica and the intelligent life forms are Photarians.

Our destination star system is just ahead, a smallish blue star containing an assortment of planets much like our own. There is only one gas giant similar to Jupiter and several rocky planets. Our final destination might seem quite alien and unlikely to harbor life, but we know differently. Photonica is a moon about the size of earth and closely orbiting its gas giant planet. One complete orbit takes about two of our earth days. Photonica spends much of its time in the gas giant's shadow so it has cycles of unimaginably bright starlight to intense periods exposed to its star. Of course the intensity also changes due to Photonicas rotation once every several hours. Not only does this result in constant light variations, but tremendous tidal stresses, constant seismic upheavals and massive storms which are endless dangers. All of this was essential to the evolution of intelligent life. Life had to keep moving to avoid massive lava flows and volcanic outbreaks, earthquakes and more, so advanced intelligence was necessary to the development of survival strategies. It is far too dangerous to land, but with our sensors we can observe from a distance.

Here are some things we already know. Life existed here on Photonica 1.4 billion years before our solar system even existed. In Photonica's early eons, life forms began within their oceans where they eventually grew light collecting appendages. A few learned to jump out of the water like our flying fish. Eventually some evolved flight and started to migrate to land for long periods to absorb and store more energy, but they had to keep on the move to find water and avoid constant tectonic hazards. Their ability to fly became a survival essential. Their wings doubled as light collectors and because of the high levels of UV light they can remain aloft for long periods, but they also spend extended periods on the ground to store energy in fat reserves. Photarians are photosynthetic creatures that developed large brains since it took a lot of smarts just to survive the hazards on this tectonically active moon. Photarians look almost human except for their wings/ photon collector appendages. They do have a nose to smell danger and for breathing in CO_2. Surprisingly they developed a mouth primarily for communicating and breathing extra CO_2 during flight. They have ears that twitch and obviously no need for teeth, but a type of tongue helps taste the air and form sounds for communications.

Life existed here billions of years before life on earth, but before we go farther, we need to know a little more about ourselves. The year is 2525 and we have recovered from what we call Dark Age 2. In the year 2037 all hell broke out on earth. The Taliban, who had gained full control over Pakistan and their nuclear capability, finally decided they would launch their weapons against Israel. None of the missiles got through but the retaliation was swift with nuclear explosions devastating the entire region. Iran was also targeted and almost simultaneously Russia and North Korea started launching. The United States responded. The result was mass destruction throughout earth's northern hemisphere and the radioactive fallout poisoned everything throughout the northern hemisphere all the way to within 80 miles of the equator. Since very little air actually moves across the equator, remaining northern survivors headed south in a mass human migration.

The nuclear winter primarily affected the northern hemisphere and left it highly radiated, cold and without food. To make a long story short, civilization was in chaos and anarchy reigned for about 250 years with only a few remaining pockets of sanity below the equator. About the year 2290 stable cultures began to emerge and by 2350 we had recovered to a technology level similar to what it was in 2037, only this time we developed the united perspective that would never let the past happen again and we must work together if human kind is to survive. After that scientific advancements exploded. We had a new togetherness and a purpose to develop all means necessary to benefit and recover humanity.

The age of cooperative redevelopment began. Computers were advanced from manipulating electrons to quantum computing with enormous increases in speed and parallel capability. We finally discovered how to store photons within a molecular matrix and retrieve them again. This photonic memory changed everything. The old computers before Dark Age 2 became as antique as vacuum tube radios. Although vacuum tube radios were some of the few electronic items that survived the massive number of EMP's in the north.

In this age, most of surviving humanity was huddled within a few hundred miles mostly south of the equator. At first, scientists could not understand why earth's temperature was not recovering from the nuclear winter as quickly as expected. After much study they made a frightening discovery. Solar output had dropped from pre Dark Age 2 measurements and Ice was advancing from both poles. After careful study they determined that a new 100,000 year cycle of ice and glaciers was beginning. The amount of carbon released during the 20th and early 21st centuries was insignificant compared to the nuclear winter blockage of energy from the sun. Therefore; the only thing possible for the human remnant was to prepare. And so began the age of cold survival that continues to this day. Today's survivors live primarily underground and burn as much fossil fuel as possible to keep our subterranean cities livable.

Now let's take a deeper look into new developments of our age. Scientists have known about the quantum properties of entangled particles. That is, their ability to instantly affect each other over vast distances without having to travel at the speed of light. Well, putting two and two together, if you save half of a group of entangled particle pairs in one molecular matrix and the other half in another, and then retrieve them at a specified rate on both ends, you can modulate them on either end and capture the results on the other end enabling instant communication over infinite distances. This breakthrough answered the obvious need for effective communications over distances of space travel that would have been impossible beyond our solar system using electromagnetic waves traveling at the speed of light. Therefore, in the year 2450 the technology was developed to split a photon and save the two entangled halves in separate molecular matrix locations. When several issues were resolved the problem of inter galactic communications was solved, although early on they had synchronization difficulty due to the fact that time changes with the speed differences between transceivers.

One development always leads to additional advancements. When quantum communications finally replaced all other methods of communications a major discovery occurred. More particles were found to be entangled. It seems that at the big bang all particles were created with multiple entanglements. New discoveries allowed our quantum computers to study minute phase, frequency and orientation in vibrations of entangled particles and determine the distance and direction of their entangled partners. We found that a significant percentage of particles have entangled mates that are spread throughout the universe by the big bang. We also found that a usable percentage are in what we call quantum clumps since the distribution is uneven. It turns out that one high percentage clump of entangled particles with mates on earth is located at Photonica. We gathered great quantities of these particles and fed them into our quantum computers and by monitoring their modulations we have been able to study every aspect and characteristic of Photonica right here from earth. In fact, we can observe all life and activity as it happens within our quantum projection theater. So today we are about to share with you what we discovered!

Returning to our story let's jump forward a billion years in Photonica time. We now have life forms that are a lot like us, only they are plant like (photosynthetic) and by far technically advanced beyond us. Biologically their wings double as large photosynthetic collectors they don't need mouths to eat with, but they have something similar that evolved for communications. They created safe living places on Photonica and have traveled and explored countless other moons and planets.

Early in their travels they encountered microbes that they had no defenses against, but their biggest surprise was animal like parasitical creatures that could attack and devour them. Their response was predictable. They were appalled because they had never encountered such violence. Parasites of any kind never evolved on Photonica. After several thousand of their years they formed coalitions with other galactic photosynthetic advanced beings and began a campaign to eliminate all parasites from our Milky Way galaxy. They have currently cleared the inner 7 Kpc and are moving out rapidly. Their collective technology is far beyond ours and we seem to be like ants to them.

They have studied humans and have found nothing of value. Everything we do is related to consuming and reproducing, causing us to fight and kill for little reason. Consuming living organisms for our survival is horrific to them. Our teeth shock and dismay them. When they observed us celebrating as we eat, they were petrified. How could we celebrate when we kill and consume innocent life forms? They consider our birthing process as gross with all kinds of nasty fluids spilling everywhere, and they think our babies are as ugly as small monsters or like baby naked rats. They refuse to encounter us directly. Not only are our teeth ghastly and our odor intolerable, but we carry all kinds of parasite microbes that are toxic to them. They think that our intense odor is why dogs can track us for days even if we just briefly pass through a place. The Photarians have studied dogs in disbelief about their adaptability to tolerate us. We consume living things then excrete large amounts of indigestible parts, a messy and foul smelling process. Our entertainment is centered either on killing or reproduction. In older times we had colosseums and gladiators with 50,000 spectators participating in death. On rare occasions, animals were allowed to maul and eat a live humans, sometimes tied to a stake. Such things and many others are despicable to the Photarians, and justifiably so. They know that we are inherently violent, even killing our own kind in mass. By studying our teeth they originally believed that we only consumed plant life like themselves, but after additional study they found that through the use of fire we were able to cause meat to have the consistency of vegetable matter and with seasonings and burnt flavors we developed a taste for it. Because we are so violent and consume other parasitical animals they believed that we would soon destroy ourselves, so they placed us on a lower priority list for elimination.

There are some far advanced galactic animal species that have given up consuming organic food years ago. These now consume only synthesized foods and have been allowed to survive by the Photarian alliances, but humans have been unable to advance to that level and time is running out.

We expect them to arrive as soon as they work their way out to our fringe of our galaxy. You can be sure of this, they are coming and there is nothing we can do about it.

Born Free

One bird in the bush
Is worth more
Than a thousand caged

One man in the bush
Is worth more
Than a thousand slaves

Where have you been today?

A powerful dichotomy

Furious power

 Impressive indeed

 But soon to go

Gentle power

 Not easily seen

 Sculpts solid stone

13. GOLDEN BALL SPECULATION

Golden balls have been found in caves under Mexico's Teotihuacan complex near the Pyramid of the Sun. So far their purpose has been called a mystery. They are made of clay and coated with golden pyrite, probably applied before firing. Pyrite is an electrically semi-conducting mineral. Also large slabs of mica have been found in the area. Mica is an insulating material used in many electronic applications. In this prehistoric period there were no wires to conduct electricity and certainly no obvious need for them. Even so, high voltage electrical current could be conducted through these semi-conductive balls insulated from the earth by thick sheets of mica. All you would need is to build channels, insulated with mica and filled with the golden balls. These are facts, now here are my highly speculative ideas. What purpose could ancient people possibly have to conduct electricity?

Pyramids have been embellished in many ways like adding the large highly polished golden top theorized to once cap the Great Pyramid of Giza. These beautiful gold tops would have been looted many years ago, but let's assume one existed here at Teotihuacan. During wind and electrical storms these precious metal tops could easily build up a high static voltage charge. Now people in those days who believed in a spiritual connection of these monuments might be tempted to climb the pyramid for a closer and godlier experience. People would also soon learn that a statically charged golden top could zap you. The probable conclusion, this is our "Plumed Serpent God" speaking, it sure feels like his bite.

People back then are just as curious and inventive as we are today. Surely someone dreamed of bringing this god's bite into their entire complex. They probably discovered that a chain of hand holders could feel this god's bite and he could pass through them to the end of the line, but that is not a practical distribution solution. Gold was in short supply since they used most of what they had on the pyramid top and other adornments. So Peat their Chief took action and called together their Engineering Team of pyramid designers and gold artisans to answer this challenge. How can we distribute this god's bite? In charge of the team was Shawn the Shaman. ;-)

So the team experimented to see what else they could find to contain and pass their god around to the entire complex for everyone to experience his love bite. Eventually someone discovered pyrite which easily passes high voltage, but how do they find enough to distribute their god to everyone? Another smart Indian expressed that it could be applied to pottery and proposed applying it to the outside of fired clay balls, then they could be lined up to carry this snake bite over the distance. To make a long story shorter, the end result of their research was mica incased channels filled with pyrite coated balls terminating at many golden images around the complex. All their people could touch them and feel the bite of the Plumed Serpent god throughout the "Avenue of the Dead" area.

This became a very popular addition to their worship time and they would wonder how is our god feeling today? One day there was a fierce dry lightning storm. The gold top on the Pyramid of the Sun received a direct hit. This powerful lightning strike exploded gold balls and set fire to everything all around the complex. They assumed that they had angered their god and afterward the entire pyramid complex was feared and abandoned.

If this is not even close to the way things actually happened that's okay, but maybe it would make a great movie! Call it "***Golden Balls***."

14. SO MUCH LEFT BEHIND

- **The cats**

Not only did I never get back to my original earth voltage/earthquake experiments, I didn't have the opportunity to apply some low voltage at various frequencies to our housecats and observe their reactions and sensitivities.

This was not a divorce issue because it never went beyond thoughts.

- **Burning Carbon**

When I was in high school I was in the garage playing with an old high voltage radio transformer. After placing the high voltage leads close enough to spark, I noticed some smoke as the insulation started to burn. All of a sudden a blinding light lit up the interior of the garage. The insulation had carbonized and created a carbon arc. That generated a lot of curiosity.

Much later, I kept thinking about why carbon arc lights contained so much ultraviolet and why they produced so much illuminating power. Carbon arc lights even lit up airplanes from the ground in WW2. Flashlights were nothing compared with this light. You can tell me that the carbon just gets that hot at the ends of the electrical spark, but this never completely satisfied me. I figured there might be some atomic activity releasing extra power and I began to wonder if more energy could be created than the amount needed to create the arc, essentially burning carbon as a source of energy.

I began to think of ways to test this theory and to increase the efficiency. I even pulled some carbon rods out of old batteries. I thought about capturing the fumes and sending some off for gas analysis. Around the same time I retired, I was involved with a home sale, I had a 5 way heart bypass operation and we moved to Utah. I was seriously distracted and I never got back to it.

- **Separating electromagnetic fields**

One day I began thinking about magnetics and voltages. I know magnets. They have electrons spinning around inside molecules which have been aligned such that the individual molecule's magnetic fields are additive, eventually escaping the body of the magnet. Voltage fields remain contained within each molecule of the magnet. You end up with a magnetized chunk of metal which is voltage neutral. I also know static voltage. As long as a voltage remains static (unchanging) it does not produce an external magnetic field. So I got to thinking. Why can't I separate voltaic fields from magnetic fields within a transmitted signal? So I decided to build an experiment and if I kept the frequency low enough I might be able to prove the concept of transmitting voltage fields and magnetic fields separately.

I built a rotating arbor containing two separate fields electrically activated through separate sets of slip rings and brushes. I used a small shielded motor to rotate the arbor at 15 Hz. (cycles per second). One section used an electromagnet to generate a magnetic field and the other was a flat double sided printed circuit board with opposite polarity dc voltages applied on separated sides, one positive and one negative. I could turn on each field separately or at the same time producing alternating north and south magnetic fields or positive and negative voltage fields.

I also built two hand-held receivers identical except for the receiving heads and some impedance matching front-end components. The magnetic receiver head was a simple coil of wire and the voltage receiver was an open air flat plate. Progressive signal strength LED arrays were provided to indicate signal reception strength. It was in 2002 when I successfully demonstrated that I could activate each field, (magnetic or voltaic), and only the intended receiver would receive and light up. Both receivers would light up if both fields were activated together.

I then started to attempt performing tests at a higher frequencies. This was when life overwhelmed me again. I eventually boxed it up and stored it away. Later I took it out and found that one of the receivers had quit working, so I boxed it back again and it is stored high up in my garage where it sits to this very day. I am tempted to take it down and take a picture, so if one appears below you will see what I originally built. I don't intend to do anything more with it. It is just another thing Left Behind.

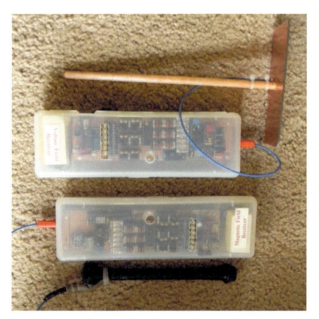 

Receivers Voltaic and Magnetic Field Generator @ 15Hz

- **Extracting Solar Energy from the Thermal Coefficient of Materials**

Why has this been missed? Heat from the sun expands and contracts nearly everything daily and these movements, although quite tiny, contain enormous potential power.

I was returning from a cross country trip and we were in the process of loading our things on a hotel cart. There was a motorcycle gang in the parking lot and one of them came by and loudly started to complain about the prices at the hotel. Looking back it was an obvious and very smooth distraction. When we were setting up in the hotel room we realized my laptop computer was missing and the motorcycle gang was long gone. After returning home I recovered much of my data, but all my design documentation on this idea I could not recover.

I had thought a lot about recovering solar energy from the expansion and contraction of materials as they were heated by the sun. I considered liquids and solids and finally decided on building a prototype using the thermal properties of stainless steel cable (SS 316 if I could find some the right size). I developed detailed drawings including the aluminum collector plates that I would take to a machine shop for fabrication. All these drawings were gone.

I decided I would someday reproduce these drawings and finish this project even though redoing the document work was not appealing. Sure, but someday does not exist, my time on earth is limited and I don't need to get rich anyway. In this life I am rich in many other ways and because of a contented life I have always lacked the motivation to spend a lot of time on any one thing. ***There is more to life than being consumed by anything and much more that I need to explore!***

So here is my challenge to everyone who reads this. You do it. I will even tell you that with my prototype design the key breakthrough was the incorporation of a mechanical differential.

- **Underground Communications**

In my lifetime many miners have been trapped underground by collapses of mining tunnels. Some have been left without communications and the ability to tell someone on the surface "hey, I'm still alive." Thinking about it, it seems that voltaic fields won't travel through the earth very well, but what about magnetism? Obviously the earth has a magnetic field and we can detect variations in that. Might it be possible to build a simple and inexpensive transmitter and receiver system using very low frequencies? I started to collect parts to build one based on 100 KHz thinking this frequency would be high enough to carry voice modulation and possibly low enough to pass through several thousand feet of dirt at low power. Of course the receiver would need to be highly sensitive. A super heterodyne may do an adequate receiving job.

Maybe it was the difficulty I envisioned with finding an available testing spot underground. Or possibly I was distracted by something else. Maybe the task would take too much of my time. I don't know really. I never got around to developing any documentation and it's just another thing here in my Left Behind chapter. I still think it was a good idea that someone should pursue. Even low frequency audio sound waves seem to travel nicely through the earth.

I just removed 102 potential development ideas from the following space in this book.

I don't have enough life, enthusiasm or energy left to pursue them anymore. However, there is one that still interests me enough to do a little more work.

- **Gravity waves**

I was reading about the latest black hole research and the thought came to me that it would sure be nice, if it could be possible, to detect gravity waves with a bench top detector instead of the miles long machines that are currently in being used. That night, while I was fast asleep, an idea woke me up instantly. So I worked out the details (in my mind) the following day. It seems impossible from the little I know about gravity, but gravity seems weird enough for me to try a new approach. A prototype will probably not have enough signal to noise sensitivity, but something completely new is always worth trying. I just must finish this manuscript first, so you will not know anything about it for now, but if it works you will surely hear something eventually. Wish me luck.

15. ANTIMATTER

Allow me to expand a little more on the subject of antimatter. Nuclear power is convenient because the energy in uranium is already stored within the mineral. We just have to concentrate and control it for use. Even in nuclear weapons it is reasonably safe because it must be compressed by a separate and precise high explosive shaped charge in order to reach supercritical and explode with nuclear power.

Antimatter has no power until it is created and all the power that it will possess must be fed into it. For example, you might have a dedicated nuclear power plant feeding energy into the antimatter creation process. Over a period of time all of that energy will be stored in a very small amount of antimatter. In military use it would contain an enormous explosive potential from a very tiny bit of antimatter. In commercial use it might be developed into a vast energy storage system. However, dangers must be recognized and mitigated. If an accident should occur and all of that power is released it would be catastrophic.

I imagine a cell phone battery that lasts longer that the phone, but if too much energy is stored within the antimatter battery it may disintegrate everything nearby. I cannot imagine systems safe enough to control antimatter either during its creation or within products, but safeguards will surely be developed and eventually antimatter storage systems will become commonplace. I suspect developing antimatter systems will be far more dangerous than "tickling the dragons tail", even without radioactivity.

Before I leave antimatter let's consider antimatter just a little closer. Every time we generate an antiparticle, an equivalent normal particle of matter is also generated. A reasonable conclusion has been accepted that at the big bang just as much antimatter as matter was created. There are still questions about whether antimatter has gravity or antigravity. Since we don't see it gathering together to make things like anti-stars and anti-planets I highly suspect that it must contain antigravity. There seems to be enough other variances to question if an antigravity universe would look anything like our own. Science fiction has speculated that antigravity worlds may exist in other dimensions or that they may exactly mirror our own. I would say that these are only possible in the movie maker's wildest dreams. It seems to me that antimatter, or what may remain of it, has to be right here within our universe, right under our noses.

Let's pretend that we have confirmed that antimatter has antigravity and other more subtle differences (like spin) that make antimatter quite unlike anything we have experienced. If antimatter has antigravity, then it could not congregate to form anything we commonly observe through our telescopes. It is more likely to be completely dispersed and repel itself into an ever expanding very thin antiparticle fog, completely and thinly dispersed throughout our vast universe and quite invisible to us. I suppose it would also be repelled by and repel the gravity of common matter and possibly produce vast empty spaces around matter while placing expansion pressure on everything. Antimatter electrons (called positrons) are speeding around at the speed of light, antiprotons can be moved around like matter. Both are being detected by cosmic ray detectors. I suspect that antimatter is much more common than detections would indicate because of the massive black hole in our galaxy opposes the antimatter antigravity and pushes much of it far away into deep space. That might be good for our local space travel.

Could it be possible that antimatter is present in our universe in a high enough volume to explain the increasing acceleration of our good old universal expansion? [**Dark energy**]

Personally, if I had the time and enthusiasm, I would like to study the merging of matter and antimatter fields in an attempt to fashion a combined and stable structure.

Anyway, if I imagine a completely dispersed antimatter spreading somewhat evenly throughout the universe it leads me to wonder how it may affect light that we observe from distant objects. Could this account for our luminosity issue in relation to **dark matter**?

It can't be a complete vacuum if space ships wear out.

Sorry,,,,, I am such a dreamer!

WISDOM

Wisdom is a disease of aging....
Unfortunately
Some seem immune for life

16. VINYL RECORDS RETURN

I love the return of vinyl records when played on a system capable of reproducing a full audio frequency spectrum. There is something very special about sharing great music with others. Even the covers are great fun to explore. But most of all it is us together.

I have a favorite Christmas Record simply called "A Christmas Album." It was recorded in 1983 by Amy Grant. I like to play it at Christmas time at least once each year. It has some beautiful music and my favorite is the first song on side 1, [A tender] Tennessee Christmas. When you open the album cover you find a snowy night scene with a warmly lit home in the background. You also find a photo of Amy with her extended family. There are 19 people ranging from baby to Grandmother appearing to enjoy each other's companionship in a warmly lit room. The music seems to come straight from Amy's heart, filled by the spirit of God and the love of her family. You can easily imagine their endearing essence when this three or four generation family gathers together. This is where I get nostalgic and think of what should have been.

Don't get me wrong, I love my life and all my family members. Our families and my faith, provides true riches. The opportunities and the joy of loving and helping others has risen out of the rubble of the past. My life now is richer and fuller than I ever experienced before, but I am dreadfully sorry for those who missed out on a strong family, filled with love, compassion and nurturing. Early days were dysfunctional from the beginning and I didn't know how to fix it.

It was like a gold plated egg that was fractured beneath the plating. It was very fragile and when pressure was applied to the outside it began to leak. Eventually the cracks became crevasses and the contents flowed out with nothing left but a broken empty shell. When a breeze came along it fell from its pedestal and shattered.

So I dedicate this book to you my children, and suggest only this. Hard boil your eggs.

Dad

LOOKING BACK

I fill my days full
I dare not stop for a moment
Folly is closing in

WORKING?

I have been very hardly working today!

17. UNFRIENDLY ORGANISMS, AMONG MAN'S GREATEST NEMESES [STARTED BEFORE COVID 19]

As mother earth's human population increases to an enormously tasty number, our greatest threat will come in the form of teaming hordes of microbes evolving into new disease species. You see, we are their live-in soup. Each new member of the human race provides one more new home within which millions of microbes will be nourished. Never before in history has so many man-munching microbes had the opportunity to evolve into new and potentially catastrophic exotic diseases. The rate of microbe evolution is increasing at an enormous rate, driven at a factor many times the rate of our own population explosion. New and drug resistant diseases are sure to outpace our ability to defend ourselves. As human population increases, the rate of newly evolved microorganisms that arrive on the scene may soon surpass our intellectual ability to create defenses. When this occurs, the world could easily experience another prehistoric-like extinction period. Only this time it will be us.

When human population was low, not only were there far less microbe factories (us), the world wide microbe distribution system was far less effective. Man lived mostly in remote isolated tribes. In the rare occurrence of the evolution of a deadly microbe, the tribe might be wiped out, but there it would end. Today however, no one is isolated from anyone. Every day we come in contact with people who have come in contact with people who have come in contact with people from everywhere on the planet. We cannot avoid it, and we cannot afford to continue to be complacent. In this age, a highly contagious and deadly microbe will find it easy to reach nearly every human on earth. When this happens, everything as we know it will catastrophically change.

Man has inadvertently created this new and highly dangerous situation. Our combined intelligence has allowed us to alter our immediate destiny by extending life spans and decreasing mortality through the temporary defeat of most common microscopic predators. This has accelerated our human population explosion and has offset a natural balance that previously existed. With such an enormous organic resource available to our microbe predators, the stage is set for impending disaster.

As I have walked through the forests and fields and observed the wide variety of flora and fauna present in local environments, over and over I have pondered the question: why is nature so diverse? On the surface, it would seem that diversity should not be the norm. Shouldn't evolution continue to strengthen each species increasing its ability to survive? And if so, why can't one species gain a complete advantage forcing all competitors into decline? If reason tells me this should happen, observation tells me that quite the opposite is the norm. What unseen forces are at work generating the vast diversity on this planet, and what is stopping every species on earth from taking over compatible environments completely? And finally, I must ask, when will these mystery forces catch up with us, cutting short our progress toward domination?

Could diversity of species be a simple response to diverse environments, or to limited resources such as space and nourishment; and is man's good fortune just because we are smart and have provided better for ourselves? I think not. Within any naturally rich ecosystem one can find a wide variety of similar plant species taking hold of small plots of ground here and there; but in the four and a half billion year evolutionary history of this planet, no species has gained a total advantage over all the others.

From observing the artificial environments that man has created, we can gain insight into what is going on. What happens when we breed and propagate vast fields of single species food crops? Due to the vast expanse and uniformity of the crop, with its limited genetic diversity, an enormous opportunity is opened for a microorganism to gain an advantage against the entire crops immune system. Many times this has resulted in total crop devastation by disease. It seems that the natural evolutionary forces to advance any single species are constantly and totally overwhelmed by predatory attacks of the outnumbering and rapidly evolving microbe population. The only possible long term survival technique is for a species to occupy isolated pockets, and better if they are genetically diverse. This condition is indeed nature's order and a state of equilibrium of which mankind is naively violating. We must recognize our plight. We must prepare for the fight of our lives which surely lies close at hand.

The warning signs are abundant. Look at what is occurring around us. Legionnaire's disease, streptococcus that melts away flesh, AIDS and various outbreaks of deadly infections throughout the world. These early warnings appear to be resulting from newly evolved microbes. Also remember the new drug resistant strains of old enemies such as tuberculosis. What if, just by chance, AIDS would have been highly contagious and airborne? The entire human race could have been infected and the majority of us eliminated. In fact, it is possible that most of humankind is at the very brink of being wiped out in short order by such a microbe nemesis. We must prepare to engage the enemy with all our scientific and intellectual resources before it becomes too late. Unfortunately we don't know where, when or how it will occur.

So you say, "this is depressing, I don't want to read any more of this stupid book!" My desire is not only to present a wake-up call, but also to stimulate renewed scientific research that may result in saving humankind. I believe that solutions are not far off if creative thinking is applied to solving the problem. The very first step is to recognize that a problem exists. Many scientists already know, but I hope that I can add enough to stimulate a political arousal.

So where do we go from here? What if a "think tank" comprised of some of our greatest scientific minds was set up to concentrate on this one problem? How many new ideas could be generated in the very first day alone? For example, could evolved defenses already be available among earth's vast biological diversity? What about mosquitoes that relentlessly spread nasties? Could they actually have evolved anti-viral defenses that are currently unknown to us? I'm sure that it would be presumptuous to say that extract of mosquito might be a good elixir, but what about vampire bats? These mammals have biological systems which are much closer to ours. Shouldn't we at least look to see how they continue to thrive on diverse and frequently diseased blood? Maybe these ideas are shallow, but I'm not qualified anyway. I'm confident that great scientific minds can come up with greater ideas if politicians give it a national priority.

The Bible tells us that there will be great plagues in the end times. Is this prophesy taking shape in our time, and if so, should we simply accept it? For what purpose does God give us our creativity and the ability to alter our destiny? I leave these questions with you for further consideration.

2020 Spring Update:

Our Species is at War!

We need to reassess our "common sense." Cities might be convenient, but their high density creates high vulnerability. Urban sprawl might be a good thing by providing space between neighbors. High density housing is very dangerous and if it continues many improvements need to be made. For example, each unit should have its own isolated entrance and I have no idea how to separate all those children at play. Mass transit exacerbates mass pandemics. A complete redesign of society is necessary with renewed research, preparation and positive actions starting now. Isolated individual transport can't be beat. What good are environmental or efficiency concerns if we are no longer here?

How long will it take before we wake up enough capable leaders to start designing our future living environments to protect and enhance the survival of our species? I don't have the answers, but a scientific approach with new directions and political will is needed. Dare we go back to sleep when this covid-19 is over? Who will fight the battle over the high cost of preparing for this new pandemic filled age? Who will develop an investigative problem solving team to create a new vision and future focused on human survival?

The microbes are not waiting!

2020 Summer Update:

Well here we are, as I expected, deep within the latest deadly pandemic. Is it airborne or not? No matter. It has turned out to be extremely contagious either way. I previously mentioned our increased human population (density) and the homogenization of our species (even DNA) through global interconnectedness. This has put us at extreme danger for contracting diseases since we are a nearly limitless host for vastly outnumbering, explosively multiplying and rapidly mutating microbes.

By far we have suppressed nature's tensions and evolutionary norms. We have found artificial ways to defeat many diseases with numerous medicines and vaccines. We have conquered the natural limitations of food supply and water availability. Overall, we have learned to avoid every attempt of nature to limit the population of our species and we have essentially overrun our entire planet. Now we are suffering from being condensed into smaller and smaller spaces for living and travel, exacerbating the certainty of living within the ever advancing microbe swarms.

My concern is this; are we approaching an unavoidable tipping point? Have we so violated the natural world that microbes have become so numerous, so adapted to mutating and so potentially lethal that we can no longer stay ahead of the fight against them? It seems that Covid-19 has already mutated once, even before a vaccine and other medications have been developed to cover the original threat. Also Covid-19 antibodies seem to diminish rapidly so it is possible for a person to redevelop the disease within months. If microbial mutations keep occurring faster than our efforts to counter them what will happen? It seems that a die-off of human population may be unavoidable and could continue until our population returns to a natural balance of small, isolated and DNA diverse communities.

If this scenario occurs a new normal will follow and we will have long passed the pinnacle of human population. Everything that we know and trust will change almost overnight and we will have very little time to find new ways to survive. What we love today may become meaningless tomorrow. Our interconnected and fragile culture is far too vulnerable as we have recently seen. Toilet paper became a vivid example. Nature has its amazing ways of rebalancing everything.

Who alone can be ready for this possibility?

I recall the communes of the 1960's and our enlightening Mother Earth News. I still have my Tassajara bread book and trusty grain grinder. Most of these communes no longer exist. Long term independent and isolated communal living may be more difficult to accomplish than it seemed in those days, but some form of this could become the necessary new norm. While our collective intelligence is still intact we need to start working to reduce this problem. If we continue to live as before, it is possible that an especially lethal pandemic or plague may soon arise reducing our entire human population toward prehistoric levels. Will we commit mass suicide by indifference or complacency?

IT'S BEST TO BE UGLY

When we've lived twenty years
We are practically here
Just starting our life we are told

But as thirty grows near
With our first new gray hair
It's too bad, we are just growing old

How sad it is dear
That we bloom ten short years
And the rest we are not worth a ham.

If I live ninety years
I'll spend eighty right here
Seeking things which I can't understand

And it's worse for those who
Are so lovely to view
Facing fear as the years slip away

When those ten have gone by
They sit wondering why
They have ended up losing their way

So in happiness be
Just as ugly as me
And find something better to do

You can bet your sweet lass
That those ten go by fast
And your mirror will make faces at you

Johnny Doubter 1980

18. I MUST BE MISSING SOMETHING AGAIN

We have been in a losing "war on drugs" since it began. As our culture loses purpose, people want more drugs to cover up anxiety, pain, depression, lack of self-worth and much more. That creates great demand, an illegal market and criminal activity. Who is seriously studying the "root causes" and attempting to correct problems before people feel they need to start self-medicating?

We need a total culture flush. I propose a massive, government funded, task force dedicated to Identifying and solving people issues. Broken homes, physical and sexual abuse, bullying in schools, lack of self-worth, boredom, fear, environment, violent entertainment and the list goes on. Instead of a country of freedom and you get what you deserve, we need a country of love, assistance, protection and guidance for everyone who is lost and struggling. When we finally get to be next in the help line we should hear, "we are going to help you now" not "oh, that problem is in handled by a building on the other side of town if you can qualify."

And then there is the biggie. How in hell's name have we allowed the opioid dealers to saturate their pills into everyday lives? Opioid pills are legalized heroin. Take a few too many and you are addicted, if not dead. Many of our countrymen continue to fall. These pills should be at the top of the illegal drug list and completely removed from our civilization. Anything less is a travesty. In small amounts they relieve pain, but we can do better by developing something that will not destroy lives in the process. Let's get on with it and off of them!

Carrying on the way we are makes no sense. Big pharma, unscrupulous doctors and purchased politicians are making big money. Adequate systems are not in place to prevent all levels of abuse. We the people must rise up and push back if none of our leaders have the backbone. As a nation we cannot continue to sustain this ongoing destruction of people's lives.

I know, much of it now is illegal on the streets, but let's start where we can.

19. SLAVES TODAY

What is freedom?

Our freedom is not something to be taken lightly. Walking to the store without covering ourselves in special clothing. Living in a neighborhood of our choice without harassment or moving elsewhere if we desire. Firmly holding and speaking our beliefs without attack. To be discerning without being labeled hateful or prejudice. Expressing our opinion without fear of being punished. Being able to worship if, when and how we choose. To be protected from the powerful, and the downtrodden. Absolute ownership of lawfully obtained possessions. To discipline your children as you see fit, within the law and within reason and without causing lasting harm; physical or mental. To move about unimpeded. To sacrifice our time and efforts and receive just compensation. To have law enforcement personnel work with you from a subservient, advocate position (Protect and Serve). To have affordable, individualized education and equal opportunities thereafter.

These are just a few things that represent my idea of freedom. There are many more and you probably know more as well. As our freedoms are eroded away, we become enslaved. Socialism is slavery on steroids.

Everyone is different and we are naturally attracted toward different things. Our first few school grades should be directed toward identifying things that naturally attract us. Therefore, young children should be exposed to the greatest variety of experiences. During this time each child should have teachers developing a comprehensive data base on likes, dislikes, skills and personality. By the end of the third grade the education should start to be focused away from general education toward being child interest focused and this should continue through high school. All US citizens should have free education as long as their course of interests plays out. Higher education schools should charge tuition only to foreign students. Computer guided education should be free and all students should have the opportunity to advance at their own rate. After grade school there should be no grades, only focused programs following the student as the student can or desires to progress.

In the future, there will not be enough jobs for people within automated industry and farming. Therefore, a culture shift needs to occur, returning to the values of hand-made goods. The virtue and value of craftsmanship must return.

Are we enslaved today? Most of us give up at least eight hours a day to become some company's slave. Not counting sleep hours because we are somewhere unknown when we sleep, work enslaves almost half our awake lives just so we can survive. Let's just call it 40% considering days off, if we are so lucky. So we are enslaved 40% of our lives to earn our existence. Therefore our money must be worth that 40% of our lives. Let's look at taxes. The Tax-Foundation tells us that all taxes absorb 30% of our income on average. That is like taking a portion of our livelihood, so I suggest it should be added to the 40% labor for a total of 70% enslavement.

Before I leave taxes I need to make one more complaint concerning "ownership" in our country. Unlike Steven Hawkins, I believe there are basic human rights. I consider ownership one of them. I own my own body, what I say, what I do, what I create and what I earn. I cannot own something for which I must continue to pay. Property tax eliminates ownership. It is a disgrace for people to finally pay off a mortgage and still continue to pay property tax. If you think you own it, just stop paying the tax and you will find out who really owns it.

Now let's consider insurance. Insurance is classic socialism. Everyone pays hoping they will never need it. We pay dearly $$$ for our socialism (insurance) in this country. Some of it is even mandatory like auto insurance. You are required to have it if you want to travel anywhere, even just to get to and from your enslavement, (work that is). To me, all insurance should be distributed through our government since it is pure socialism. That is, if we had a government we could trust to distribute money prudently.

Do you want a home, utilities, food and all the stuff that consumes life, even our time? It is easy to see that just to live the remaining 30% is also completely consumed. I haven't even mentioned the cost of higher education.

Blink and our lives are gone and we don't know why. We need a complete culture reset to gain our freedom back, but what are we willing to give up to get it back? It is time for a complete culture restructure and just possibly a little of our freedoms can be recovered.

Oops, I also forgot how much commercials steal from our few moments of rest. I thank God for my mute button, but I wish it was a complete commercial killer.

Realize this, liberty erodes over time and we hardly notice. I just read that a little town in Florida is fining seniors tens of thousands of dollars and bankrupting some for muni code infractions. This is shameful. Many new laws may seem right. We all might like a neat and tidy neighborhood to live in, but we don't always see how much of our own freedom is being dwindled away. I believe every law should automatically terminate after 10 years and re-justifying each one could give lawyers something righteous to do. Before reenacting any new law it must be compared to our constitution and our liberties. If we own property we should be able to do whatever we decide is right in our own eyes unless it actually harms others. Today that would be revolutionary, but it would bring forth a burst of long lost freedoms and a renewed excitement for our founding documents. For instance, we should be able to modify our home any way we see fit. If we sell it, inspectors should only describe safety, security and condition issues to the buyer. If the buyer is okay with the findings it should become a legal sale. We need a system of laws that promote liberties and not where liberties are continually diminished. **Don't try to tell me that we are not Slaves!**

I don't know how to fix this. Private companies have so much fine print they can wiggle out of almost anything. People think they are covered until something happens. All natural disasters need full coverage.

PS: Why are children in TV commercials exempt from child labor laws? Many must be terribly abused, if not physically then psychologically and driven by parents for the love of money.

We are already Socialism saturated! We are **The United Socialist States of America (USSA).**

THERE SHOULD BE A LAW

Laws replace thoughts and opinions
When there are enough laws
To regulate all opinions
Thinking will be outlawed

20. IN THE AGE OF FOLLY [A MESSAGE FROM OUR FUTURE]

In the past:

People could dangerously drive a car or fly an airplane manually

Affordable houses were built with flammable materials

Some folks owned their own home, although more likely a bank or development lord

People were allowed to take plastics and other dangerous flammable poisons into their homes

It was legal to jump or swing from of high places and many other dangerous activities were legal

There were still a few free TV and radio stations available

They could do what they wanted on their own property, without totalitarian municipal control

They could still own a few things without paying the "forever tax" on all ownership

It was still legal to resist injustices

People received a salary based on the value they provided

Minimum wages were not so high that almost everyone became poor

People were not held responsible for what their ancestors did

The location of every human was not tracked by satellite and highly controlled

All devices were not tied into our "Big Brothers Data Web in the cloud"

People were not assessed before entering anything and everything

They had a right to own guns, knives, chain saws and many other dangerous things

Self-defense was not a crime

They still could go hunting and fishing

Eating meat was not considered cruelty and some animals even worked and entertained

The government didn't ration and charge for every drop of water and every cubic meter of air

There were still places they could freely choose to travel without authorization

Children were allowed to play and explore, and parents had authority over them

Education was not programmed, uniform and propagandized

Gender was still acknowledged and flirting was not a criminal act

The news media could be trusted, and it provided more than propaganda and advertising

The government did not confiscate everything for our (so-called) fair and even redistribution

Ours was considered a Christian nation and Christians could travel safely and unimpeded

People could say "Merry Christmas" without being criminalized

It was still legal to become special or even extraordinary

Occasionally opinions were valued and rationally considered without inciting mob violence

Religious beliefs and discernments could be voiced without being arrested for prejudice or hate

In those days no one could be arrested for their thoughts, which are now monitored and controlled

Christian religion was alive and was a source of love, compassion, morality and human rights

Accountability was a virtue and in those days and responsibility still meant something

A nationalist was just someone who loved our country and being white was not a disgrace

Politicians were to know what our constitution provides and were required to deliver it for the people

Escaping the anxieties of society and government was possible, if only for a moment here and there

Maybe some things were not so bad, **"In the Age of Folly"**

21. ECONOMICS 101

What is missing here? Everyone should know that if you have a bank account and you continually withdraw more than you deposit you will eventually "pay the price of bankruptcy." It is the same with our national debt. In the past we could print more money and absorb it through inflation, but we no longer have the industrial tax base to support us. Look at it simplistically. High wage jobs have almost disappeared, prices keep rising and college graduates are wondering how they will ever survive without moving back home.

Here are some facts as of December 2018: **and Update February 2021**

- Our US National (governmental) Debt is at 21.9 trillion dollars and increasing at approximately one million dollars every 36 seconds. **Update 2021: 27.8 trillion**
- Our US Total US Debt is at 71.7 trillion dollars and increasing at approximately one million dollars every 12 seconds. **Update 2021: 82.3 trillion**
  Source: http://www.usdebtclock.org/
- US population gain is about one person every 14 seconds.

Obviously our country, that has lost its industrial tax base, is going to continue "paying the price."

In the past our outgoing money has brought the economies of many countries out of poverty and into economic health. Europe after WW2, Japan and S Korea are good examples, but these investments were relatively small in comparison to our gigantic industrial base. Now we are trading with China and we are massively losing the trade imbalance.

We have done it to ourselves. During the 1990's I constantly heard from industry leaders "Offshore, Offshore, Offshore." Wealthy Americans decided that they could make a lot more money if they had their products manufactured in countries with cheap labor. So off went our high paying jobs. Our "Freedom Traitors" loved it. Product profit margins went from approximately 20% for American made goods to 80% for foreign made goods and our government did nothing to stop it. Along with manufacturing our trade secrets and highest technology equipment went out of country to support foreign factories. Now we are enriching communists. Our country sent us to Viet Nam and 86 thousand young soldiers died. Will we ever learn? When Bill Clinton made China our "most favored trading partner" I was shocked and appalled. Technical advancements occur in manufacturing plants. Not many advancements are achieved bussing tables.

When you send out lots of money, especially, but not exclusively due to trade, you hope for a fair return (fair trade). It only works like that if the money you pay for in goods and services balances with money returning into our country. When it doesn't you have a constant drain on every citizen. Our economy was strong during our industrial revolution. We were able to absorb the enrichment of smaller countries. But this is no longer the case. China is much larger than the USA and now we made it into an industrial giant.

Our train ride toward economic destruction is irreversible unless we can stop all the money leaks.

Look around and you can see the results of our enormous deficit. More than half the Hawaiian Islands are foreign owned. Large tracks of land across our country are foreign owned. Many of "our" remaining companies and industries are foreign owned. Even many of our mortgages are foreign owned. What do you expect foreigners to do with all that excess money? They have gone a long way toward buying us out. Soon there will be nothing left of our country or our lives. What a shame to trade our country for plastic toys and believe we are richer in the process. Those who have profited at our countries demise should be tried for treason.

Since we are no longer creating wealth (except for a few points of light) our huge government keeps absorbing more of us. I heard this morning that California is considering taxing cell phone texts. Will our government ever stop absorbing everything you and I have, and everything we do? I can see a day coming that we will be taxed if we walk, breathe or even sing. Every liberty we thought we had will be gone, absorbed for the "good of all (socialism)". I will be happy to be dead by then. Patrick Henry and I will receive our final wish.

When we get here, taxes will surely follow!

Socialism is slavery and has absorbed us. Capitalism was freedom until traitors sent our jobs out of our county. Very little joy remains and our country has become a Paper Tiger.

2020 Update:

WOW. If you think we were in trouble before, what do you think will be the result of printing trillions of dollars to recover from the Covid-19 pandemic? This is not going to be pretty!

22. IMPLICATIONS OF TOMORROW'S TECHNOLOGY

(I started this years ago and much is still valid)

Very soon we will be faced with some very difficult decisions. Is it of utmost value to maintain what privacy we have left or will we be willing to give up too much in the name of reducing crime? It won't be long when we will be faced with the ability to track every person on earth full time. We will be constantly monitored and recorded by satellite and integrated land based systems which will report the exact location of every human on earth. The advantage is obvious. No more lost or kidnapped children. It will be impossible to defeat the system and anyone who attempts to defeat the system will be immediately picked up. If any crime is committed the system will be able to report everyone who was near the scene and at what time. If an effective system such as this is placed in service, physical crime against people and their property will be nearly eliminated. It seems that this will be recognized as well worth the small loss of privacy. Additionally, the system would be used to constantly monitor the whereabouts of criminals who are serving time. Nonviolent criminals would no longer require expensive jail cells, they will be required to live within very limited boundaries, essentially incarcerated within their own residence, losing their rights to move freely until their sentence is completed. They would be required to work and to support themselves saving our country with more than enough money to pay for the entire system.

Violent criminals will be imprisoned. To be a real deterrent, prisons must be seen as horrible places to be. I recommend high technology prisons which keep each prisoner separated in near isolation with no contact with other inmates, guards or the outside world. Very sturdy robots will do all the interface with prisoners. Sentences may be shortened to reflect harsher conditions. Let's put an end to the prison structure which permits prisoners to socialize and learn how to do worse things while they are on the inside enjoying their comforts and privileges. AI will help generate recovery programs and personality evaluations must be accomplished before any release is granted.

Major advancements will occur in the area of travel. Personal transportation will greatly improve although less of it will be necessary with tele-commuting and shopping through the home computer. Even so, compact self-flying, computer guided vehicles will replace many, if not all self-driving automobiles. They will also be connected into master computer systems that control all vehicle movement. Individual flying vehicles will have some obvious advantages. They won't need more and more highway funds, they can travel in three dimensional space reducing congestion and they will elevate travel and exploration to a new level of excitement. So let's get to work. I'm ready to fly.

Another great advancement in transportation will be the so called Hyperloop. Large diameter evacuated tubes will stretch coast to coast. Magnetically elevated and propelled space trains will travel both directions inside these tubes. If a container is sealed like a spacecraft, it will be able to carry people and cargo from coast to coast in about an hour. Since the craft will be essentially flying in space (a vacuum) space travel speeds will be attainable without the effects of air friction. The craft would accelerate for the first half of the trip and decelerate for the second half, reaching speeds of about six thousand miles per hour at the center of a coast to coast trip. The cost to operate the craft would be very advantageous over conventional travel since there would be no friction to overcome and the energy invested in the craft to bring it up to speed will be extracted during the braking phase. It may seem like this project is too big to be possible, but look back at the challenge that the railroads took on in early America. Obtaining and maintain a vacuum could be a problem, but I have answers if anyone ever cares enough to ask.

Now I feel that I must issue some warnings. As I see it fusion is our best bet for the answer to our energy needs of the twenty first century. We must rigorously pursue this potentially endless source of energy to supply our needs. But beware, all sorts of abuses are sure to come about. We must be very careful to control and equitably distribute this new source of great power.

The rotation of the earth could be a source of power which mankind may be tempted to tap. Already some energy is being extracted from natural tidal forces. We must pass worldwide moratoriums against this temptation before any harm can be done, for all life on earth is dependent upon a relatively steady rotation rate of our earth. Above the ocean tides are great atmospheric tides which are the source of air currents and all weather patterns on earth. These are already being tapped. To reduce the rotational rate of earth is to also affect rainfall. If the earth's rotation slows enough; rain, and with it, terrestrial life will be severely impacted. So it is up to the only intelligent creatures here to maintain earth rotating at an acceptable rate.

Only now, can I share this with you. Someone is bound to think of it even if I remain silent. If extremely large low friction gyroscopes were constructed, the earth's rotation could drive the rotation of the gyroscopes and power could be extracted from the earth's rotation. May this never be done! May it be known today that we must plan for and do the exact opposite. That is, after we harness the power of fusion and other atomic energy conversion systems, we would be extremely wise to reverse the gyroscopic process that I described, driving the gyroscopes with fusion reactors and putting energy back into earth's rotation causing our day/night rotation to speed up. This will increase rainfall and reduce the potential collapse of natural terrestrial life on earth. It does seem possible to me that the lush history of prehistoric earth may have enjoyed much shorter days and nights and a much wetter weather for I've been told that the earth continues to slow in rotation due to the resistance of natural tidal forces.

One problem which is sure to get much worse before it gets better is global pollution. Although our country seems to be more aware and willing to take some action, what about all of the emerging third world countries which we love to purchase those cheap goods from? Few have the resources or resolve to be concerned about the poisoning our planet. Into the early twenty first century we will be forced to purify our air before we breathe it or face a much shortened life span. The entire atmosphere and all of the oceans will come dangerously close to being completely unable to support life. Our homes will need to be completely sealed with air purification systems which will artificially add oxygen and filter out poisons as the air is allowed to circulate inside. Transportation vehicles will also be sealed and contain similar systems. People will become more physically isolated because of environmental dangers and the need to minimize the spread of new and dangerous diseases. Technology will provide alternatives to direct physical contact with advanced video visitation rooms and virtual reality contacts with others. Virtual reality sexual encounters will challenge our morals. Many people, if not most, will work at home. Human life will increasingly need technology just to be sustained and we will completely lose the ability to survive in a wild and natural world if one existed anywhere. We will become desperately isolated and unable to enjoy much of the former beauty of planet earth. If you don't like the sound of this, then you better join me in sounding the alarm. This is a fast moving and powerful train and I don't know if enough resolve exists to stop it. We can't psychologically survive. Just remember, CO_2 is not a pollutant and is needed for life.

23. WHAT IS REAL ANYWAY?

If I'm going to take on this subject I will need to share with you much of my most personal self. In doing so I will become extremely vulnerable and open to ridicule and doubt. But there is no other way for me to help you understand my deeply personal reasons for believing much of the way I believe, and why I have chosen the path that I am on. What I intend to share with you is as true and as accurate as my recollection. Nothing has been added or taken away to make the story better. My life has been bizarre enough without the need for exaggeration.

Unlike most people who cannot remember beyond a certain age, I can remember all the way back. Believe It or not, my memory begins just before I entered my mother's womb and has very few gaps from that time forward. I don't know why this is true for me. All I know is what I can clearly recall and have shared with family members all my life as soon as I could talk. The first thing that I remember is being a formless consciousness. It seemed that I had been elsewhere and knew another life, but prior time is very shadowy. There was a presence with me, but I saw no one and heard nothing. I was very angry and I knew I had no control over what was happening. I realized that I was about to pass into something new and for some unknown reason I had an extreme desire not to give up everything from my past and the current situation as if it would be of some value later. As I moved closer to what was to come. I was inside something like a tunnel which appeared like a grey, but not threatening cloud. I had no fear, but I had an overwhelming desire to hold on to whatever memories I could as I passed from one existence into another. It's as if I knew something about what was going to happen, but I wasn't in control and I certainly wasn't in any mood to cooperate. I would hold on even if it was just the remembrance that there had been something before. And so I entered through the cloud tunnel and held on to anything I could with extreme determination. In an instant I was through and extremely pleased with myself because I had pulled through the knowledge that I had left another existence and at least remembered something of the event. Immediately I saw my mother from far above and as I was descending toward her I entered a warm comfortable place within her. I knew that I must act very quickly so I immediately implanted the whole event permanently into however many memory cells existed at that time, making absolutely certain that I would never, ever forget what just happened. I must have felt that it might be useful for something but I didn't know what. Once I had done this I was finally able to relax and was very pleased with myself. Looking back at the event, I believe that I unintentionally initiated my memory at that very moment, making it impossible for me to fall back into forgetfulness from that moment forward. I had to wait quite a while before I was born and I somehow knew, and was very comfortable and pleased with myself. So, once I had accomplished my goal of implanting the event into memory, I was able to relax and enjoy the comfort and protection of my mother's womb for quite some time.

I have a vague memory of my birth, but clearly recall that I was excruciatingly cold for a few moments. I was very uncomfortable until I was wrapped up and became warm again. The next thing I remember very clearly is when my mother brought me home from the hospital and took me into downtown Weaverville to show me off to her friends. That was a frightening experience and I screamed a lot. First of all, she had me in a baby buggy with one of those partial coverings that flopped back and forth. I remember it was dark blue and had little white tassels all around the edge. When it hid my view of mom I felt very much alone and afraid. I didn't like it one bit so I screamed. Anyway, what was also frightening were strangers sticking their huge faces down to peer in at me, one after another. The absolutely worst thing that happened was when an old gruff man picked me up. He was rough skinned, hadn't shaven for some time, had tobacco stains on his teeth and some running down his face. He smelled atrocious, probably from smoking and chewing. I was horrified. Years later I described this incident to my mother and she recalled everything. She told me "oh, that was Mister Fetser."

I have no intention of boring you with my first bee sting at 2, the time my mother got chased by the bear, the incident with mom and the rattle snake or any of the other trivial events before the age of three, but when I was about four an event occurred that would cause me to forever look upon life with great skepticism. This is what I wrote about the incident many years ago.

My Miracle

It's a brisk and brilliantly bright winter day in Weaverville, California. I cannot wait. Exploration of my world must continue. My mother bundled me up so tight that my arms no longer hung by my side. I was off. "Don't go near the pool Johnny!" [It was a concrete duck pond my dad had built]

What a magnificent sight as my toy ship sails smoothly across the sparkling surface. I must get it back, but the breeze only plays with my impatience.

I reach... I stretch... Just a little farther...

The cold liquid engulfs me. No bottom... No top... Face down and no one near... Bundled up tightly as if in a womb, I have no fear... I relax... Then all turns black...

"Now how can this be", you ask? Dead people don't write poetry! I should have died on that day and why I did not, I hardly could say. And though you may never believe, it did happen this way faithfully.

I opened my eyes and to my surprise, I was about eight feet above the earth and descending rapidly.... Now this seemed a little unusual even for a boy of four years.... My left foot made contact.... Then I was running toward the house.

Through the door I went. My father laughed but my mother, with great concern, whisked me off to get me out of my wet clothes.

In a way it seemed quite natural.... And how quickly it was over.... Might it have been a dream?

No.... And it will never be over.... For now I know, but what is real anyway? When I was a little older I told my parents what happened, and my sister, and anyone who would listen.

In my life I have experienced a number of incidents that cannot be explained by science or physics. I cherish each of them for without them I may have never pursued a spiritual direction in my life. Considering all that I have experienced, I was forced to look beyond my mortal senses for answers to questions about reality, but spiritual enlightenment didn't happen immediately. I must admit that I floundered for many years seeking answers to questions and looking for something to fill the reasoning vacuum.

I have another incident I want to share with you. Not because I want to cause anyone to think that I am anything special. Not at all, because I thoroughly believe I was completely out of control. During my first marriage I had a young family and we had been cooped up in the house enduring several days of constant rain. When Saturday morning came, for the first time in quite a while the sun was shining. I suggested that we take the old 17 foot motorhome to Big Basin Redwoods State Park which was a short distance from home. When we arrived and drove down the familiar windy road toward the campground I was amazed by the amount of water all around. A tiny meandering stream that I had seen many times had turned into a

69

raging river that sounded like Niagara Falls. I purposely parked in a space across the street from this obvious danger and told my two children they could play outside, but not to cross the street or go anywhere near that torrent of water. After feeling that the kids were safe and I could watch them out the window, I settled inside with a cup of coffee.

It wasn't long before I heard blood curdling screams coming from some distance outside. Without thinking I jumped to my feet and sprung through the door. On a dead run I observed my two kids safe where they were supposed to be, but I was still running. A little girl first came into view on the river side of the road, maybe 50 to 75 yards downstream. She was at the bottom of an eroded muddy cliff 15 to 20 feet straight down halfway in the water and clinging to a root that had been exposed by the torrent. The water was pulling at her and I started to think what can I do? I have no rope, but the answer came surprisingly fast. As I was trying to stop I must have encountered something quite slippery, possibly wet moss. Immediately both feet went straight into the air and down the cliff into the water I went, feet still in the air and completely out of control. At that point in my life I had not learned to swim. However, I don't remember my head going under water. As I floated downstream the water turned me around and back toward the bank and I spotted the little girl. For the first time I started to feel the bottom. I struggled to gain some footing as the water continued to push me toward the girl and as I got closer I began to gain a little control. The water pushed me several feet past the girl, but now I was able to force myself against the current and was able to grab some of the exposed roots the girl was hanging onto. I grasped roots on both sides of the girl and said something to calm her. I told her that we would be able to climb out, but she needed to follow my directions. One muddy place to step and one root to grasp. One at a time and we slowly made our way up the near vertical cliff. About half way up I spotted two teenage girls at the top. One was holding onto something, probably a small tree or bush and she was holding the hand of the other who had her other arm stretched toward us, but she was very far away. I told them to get back. I was afraid they would fall in and be swept away themselves. After much careful climbing we finally made it to the top. The teenagers and the little girl embraced and headed down the road while I returned the other direction back to the motorhome. Later the teenagers came to thank me, but I never saw any parents.

It was immediately obvious that from the moment I slipped I was completely out of control. I should have died again, but something more than natural life has to be going on. Someone might say it was my guardian angel. Someone might say maybe God. But no one can tell me that it just accidentally happened that way or that I did something or was worthy of anything.

Later in life I have looked at all of the many times that things could have gone just a little different and I would have perished. Eventually I heard about multiple universes and wondered if I did die in many different universes, but the one I am in now is the only one that I survived until now. After becoming a Christian I even wondered if this somehow relates to how we have "free will." I can only believe this, "something very mysterious is going on and it is orders of magnitude beyond anyone's comprehension." I could write another book.

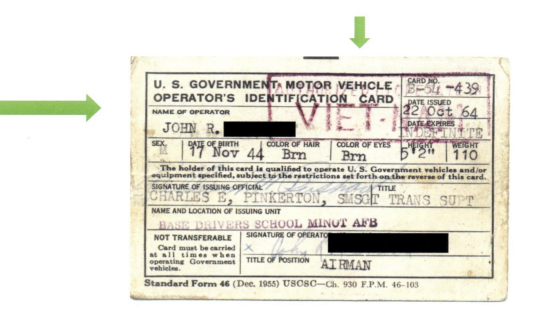

As I see it, each of us must decide what we are going to believe and for the most part we accept that which seems or feels right. In some ways to deny God and all other things that cannot be detected by our physical senses can make us feel OK for a time and is certainly easy and safe. After all, if God is real it means that we must deal with Him at some point and that does not sound comfortable. To whom or what must we deal with if there is no God? My brother-in-law used to say "when you're dead you're dead and there is nothing left," but that is not comforting. Such a philosophy completely ignores a vast area of the human existence which may be more important, more real and is certainly far bigger than the limited universe which we explore within the physical realm. When faced with this choice, I finally had to consider if being a scientific purist seems absolutely right to me. Because I had to consider all of my life experiences, the answer I got back was that without any doubt something much bigger is definitely going on. My biggest challenge was how in the world can I relate with something that is so completely concealed and untouchable?

Considering all things very carefully I concluded that it is highly unlikely that I am really here within a purely physical universe, in the flesh, at just this point in the vast time/space continuum. So I examined the options. Am I a member of a much farther advanced species who has developed to the degree that we enter into direct brain interconnections with a super computer and are taken over by this human/earth virtual reality simulation program? This would be very safe and very exciting source of entertainment for such an advanced creature. There may be a vast assortment of program options with unimaginable life forms, unimaginable laws of physics and endless worlds and conditions to choose from. Through the process, many and possibly endless lives might be lived and experienced. I can easily see mankind advancing to this level of technology in the not so distant future. So, if it can easily be imagined by me today, it must be much more likely that this is already going on instead of what I sense and perceive. I must have selected a program with technology close enough to have caught on to the fact that I am really within this simulated life just for my own entertainment.

So that is what you believe you say. Not at all! It's simply that I believe the virtual reality program simulation model is much more probable than the physical world that I perceive and can scientifically demonstrate to my mortal senses. Like everything in this life I had to judge this model against that which seems to be right. What a desperate existence it would be if the virtual reality simulation model was reality. What it would mean is that everything that I perceive is created for me and absolutely nothing is real. I dislike thinking like this, for if it is so, everything is completely meaningless. If I don't really exist, there is no purpose, so why should I even continue to write this book. This violates the rule that I predetermined which is that there must be a significant purpose to life. Mere entertainment is not enough of a purpose and therefore, I reject this simulation idea.

Well then what about this? We are just as science says, biological machines which have evolved from the survival of the fittest. Our brains are simply complex computers which have become more and more intelligent to increase our chance of survival. No matter how complex we make computers, even if we make one someday that completely simulates human behavior and we program it to claim that it is alive, I will be unable to accept that it has anything like a human self-aware spiritual essence. That is, the eternal sprit-being we perceive inside our heads. I have a definite sense of being. I am something more than a bunch of transistors programmed to say that I am alive. I am here! If you take cells from my body and clone me, the clone will never be me and I will never be the clone. Might we be spiritual beings from who knows where that have entered these empty shells of biological life just for the experience or for some other unknown purpose?

Good, so that is what you believe you say? Not at all! Even though this seems more likely than pure physics, I see no evidence. So what is really real? Must I look back to science for the answer? As scientists learn more and more and have probed the quantum realm, even they express some doubt that there is any deep underlying reality, and most consider the search fruitless. Some quantum physical phenomena are so bizarre that they destroy the core of scientific theories that we have come to rely upon. Things like a photon that is split and the two halves sent off in two directions still appear to somehow remain linked together, for if one half is simply observed, the observance causes other photon half to respond instantly, regardless of the distance between the two. That's right, instantly over any distance without waiting for the speed of light! Could there be additional unknown dimensions where things that are changed in our dimension remain unchanged? Might these dimensions influence each other? Well OK, now I am getting a little crazy. So I'll just say no! Science cannot entice me back into believing that someday they will have all the answers. Scientists are doomed to forever generate new questions.

There are endless philosophical possibilities. The great number of world religions, cults and the parapsychology followings demonstrate it. It would be simple to dream up any number of answers to explain that which we cannot contact with our senses. If it seems right, or makes you feel good for a time, it is sure to develop a following. But the problem is that in the end most of them will all leave you cold, disillusioned, desperate and empty. Many will hold fast to an empty belief right to the end with the fear of having nothing else to cling to. As long as the majority of the populace continues to become increasingly spiritually lost social decay will continue. This desperate trend must be reversed.

One thing that I have always believed is that whatever reality is, it must have a very significant purpose because the design is too elaborate and too productive to have no purpose. And if this life has a higher purpose, there will be clues along the way to act as guidepost for the direction we should take. Well, they have been here, but little did I know how difficult it would be to follow. If I would have only understood sooner how fulfilled my life would become after I yielded it completely and pursued a connection with God.

Well now, many of my evangelical Christian friends might say "now you've got their attention it's time to close the deal. It's time to tell them about Christ and how he died for us so that all who believe in him may have everlasting life". No, though a noble purpose, my desire is only this; to let you know that I have found a way that seems right to me and that it has been reaffirmed by my own changed life and by the many obvious works of God within my life.

I desire to challenge the scientist to explore an expanded world of thought and to open their minds toward being receptive to the kind of belief that produces a full and joy filled life. I fully accept science as God's creation and the Bible as God's guidance for us. Any apparent conflicts are due simply to our lack of comprehension. If God tells me that 1 + 1 is three I will say thank you lord, show me how this can be.

Once I was seriously lost. I thought I had control over life until my first marriage fell apart for reasons that cannot be explained except that it needed to play a significant role in my own spiritual growth. Very few have enough willpower and courage to surrender their lives until they are torn asunder and shown that they cannot keep life under control on their own. Well it took me until I was completely empty before I was ready to reach toward God and be filled. I wish to spare you from calamity and I wish to spare our country and our children's future from an emptiness that sucks life away.

The remainder of this chapter outlines answers which I have settled upon as the philosophical foundation for my life. These philosophies have established purpose and fulfillment in my life beyond anything that I ever thought possible. If the majority of the people could accept them the world will become a much better place for all.

I cannot accept science and physics as the answer to everything, but is there anything that can lead me to closer to truth? I know that I have never been alone, and I know that I have always received direction and protection from somewhere unseen, but when I yielded my will completely and said "OK Lord, show me the way", I was astounded with the new course my life took.

I wish you God's speed and grace in your spiritual quest. Science tells me that the earth is 4.5 billion years old and that dinosaurs roamed the earth 150 million years back and I believe that to be true. Philosophy tells me that I really cannot prove that anything was here even yesterday. All things, including my brain and it's memory and the knowledge it contains, just as it exists right now, could have been created moments ago and there would be no way to know it or to prove it. So I have settled upon the teachings of Jesus Christ and he forms a firm foundation from which I can explore this fantastic universe. When you read his teachings, you will discover that he had powerful spiritual and supernatural connections and if people could truly follow his teachings the world would become a place of peace and love.

In my quest for reality, I cannot accept philosophies, religions or new age movements that lead nowhere. If we must live as blind parasites we are doomed to endless meaninglessness. To me the answer is obvious, I must converse with the creator to find reality. Only when I meet with God will I be able to see clearly. There is only one way that I have found that provides a path to God himself, and that way is Christianity. And so, I have put my faith in Jesus and accepted him as Lord of my life. Then I will see clearly, but until that time I will provide evidence of his work to help you understand the viability of the path to Him. As for me, I can no longer imagine remaining in darkness. I depend only on the promise of Jesus documented in the bible at John 14:1-3 (NIV) it states: "Do not let your hearts be troubled. You believe in God; believe also in me. My Father's house has many rooms; if that were not so, would I have told you that I am going there to prepare a place for you? And if I go and prepare a place for you, I will come back and take you to be with me that you also may be where I am."

The beauty of a special lady is in her smile
But passion lasts for a very short while
A wise man creates her endless smiles
And beauty touches together lives

24. REDSHIFT WORRIES

There is something that really bothered me years ago! In my junior college Introduction to Astronomy class (thanks to the GI bill) my teacher told me that the big bang occurred about 15 billion years ago. He also told me that some stars appear to be about 40 billion years old according to the way they were measuring back then. Of course, this story has changed now. Anyway, as a result I started questioning redshift and how it relates to the expansion of our universe.

Heresy! Throw that vermin out! Well maybe.

Sometimes I do wish that I had more formal education because it seems to me Einstein's relativity equations may have helped me to understand a lot of things better. Gravity bends the direction of light. The gravitational lens is an accepted phenomena predicted by Einstein and verified by observations in more recent times. If gravity distorts light, it seemed to me that the total gravitational pull of the universe may also alter its apparent speed, as observed by us. Of course we know that the speed of light must remain constant relative to us. Therefore, if the speed of light is altered by the overall gravitational field of the universe, the appearance of light relative to us might be shifted in frequency dependent upon the time and distance spent within the overall universe's gravity before it reaches us.

I visualize the universe somewhat like I visualize a black hole only with very weak overall gravity. A black hole has so much concentrated gravity that light cannot escape. Presumably it slows and falls back inward. Thinking about this blows my mind. What would light appear like if we could be on the inside peering out? Might our universes' overall gravity lightly distort redshift in a similar but miniscule way depending on distance?

Anyway, it seemed to me that the speed of light or redshift from distant places within our universe could be warped by the overall universe's gravity. If so, might this cause variations in redshift readings even without considering the expanding Doppler affect? Now I've entered the world of wild speculation, but it's a fun question to ponder anyway. Maybe a scientist of sound mind can help me out of this mess that I've got myself into and inform me that the overall universe gravity is self-nullifying or these things have already been calculated into the algorithms. *After writing this and now going back and proposing antimatter with antigravity dispersed throughout our universe I have confounded myself.*

I just hope that you go easy on me so I will not be too embarrassed by your rebuke. I am sure I have missed a lot being undereducated, but very curious.

PRAISE

He's really not bad and he's really not good
As most he drifts in between
We'll try to make him act as he should
But to him we're just being mean
We can yell and scream or show him the way
He'll never recall in the end
But tell him how he did great on this day
And I'll bet he'll do it again

25. MISSING THE GREATEST GENERATION

When I was a very curious child I was fascinated by electricity and radio. I knew nothing when mom said the radio stations I listened to, in front of that big noisy box, came out of the air. Life changed when I was four when my dad, with his supervision, let me replace a broken plug on a radio. He told my mother that I did it as well as he could. That started everything and the folly of praise, pride and even at that age back then, high anxiety. Using my wood burning iron I once soldered a 115 volt power cord to a 6 volt doorbell and plugged it into house power to see what would happen. It was a very loud and a sensory exciting experience.

My dad and mom were divorced when I was 5. My single mother fell and hurt her back and never worked again when I was about 7. My sister who was nine years older than me married at 16. Eventually mom & I moved in with my sister Ramona and her husband Richard. We were very poor and I remember once living in an old teardrop trailer out in an open field, mom and I on one side with Ramona and Richard on the other. I also remember moving constantly, probably because we could not make rent payments. I remember one rental with an old barn out back. Richard somehow got hold of a table saw and some wood and the family worked together to make redwood planters. I was tiny and looked much younger than I was, so I was elected to walk door to door selling these redwood planters. I didn't know it then, but those sales kept us fed for a time.

When I was about eight we had a neighbor who worked on radios and he would let me hang out while he worked. One day he was salvaging an old set and was ready to throw away the chassis. I asked him if I could have it. He said "it just contains components," but he relented. I played with the parts and remember salvaging the speaker, and with a battery I was able to make lots of noise.

When Walt Disney came out with the book "Our Friend the Atom" mom bought it for me and I read it cover to cover many times. Because we moved so often and the schools did not follow the same curriculum I was hopelessly lost and left behind. Because of this and persistent bullies, I always looked forward to the next move. I grew to despise and even fear school.

When I was about to start middle school mom married Tony, a very strict retired Portuguese man. Don't get me wrong he taught me how to use his rototiller that made me physically strong, but he and I did not get along. During middle school I was reading every Electronics Illustrated, Popular Electronics and Popular Mechanics that I could get. I was making crystal radios and could not wait to get my hands on one of those new 2N107 or CK722 germanium transistors. Once I got one I made a 300 mw transmitter and tuned it just above the broadcast band. Some other boys and I had a lot of fun with it, but I am not willing to say how. Anyway, my stepfather and our relationship did not improve, so when I was ready to enter high school mom arranged for me to return to live with Ramona and Richard.

By that time I was completely rebellious about school. I had to be there, but that was it. I figured that if they could teach me something while I was there, fine, but when not at school that was my time and I would not study or do homework. Things like shop classes interested me and I aced every one except electronics shop. On the first day the teacher told the class that anyone who did not complete their homework would fail his class. Well, I guessed I would fail this class, and I did. Even so, electronics became my life's work.

I seem to recall California achievement tests were called Iowa tests in those days, if I remember correctly. I remember making a 97% on natural science background, but because of my terrible school record no one said a word to me. I guess I am still carrying a grudge about that. College was never even mentioned in our home and I wouldn't qualify anyway. We were way far from that social class.

After failing out of high school, I decided to get serious with my life. I took tests to join the Air Force and maxed the electronics and mechanics with an 85% in general and a 65% in administration. They gave me my choice of fields so I chose electronics and missile guidance and received training in both. I became so serious about it that I also took a correspondence electronics course in the barracks at night while others left to do what young military service boys do in town. So I absorbed everything and began a lifetime of questioning and being unfulfilled by answers that didn't always make complete sense to me.

Now back to the Greatest Generation.

I met John & Sue during my high school folly. Their oldest daughter was a buddy's girlfriend. They were a combined family. John had six daughters and a son, and Sue had one daughter and a son. Their previous marriages had been completely dysfunctional, abusive and dangerous; so their marriage was a new beginning for them with a huge focus on the welfare of their children. John had a good trade job as a glazier and worked very hard to provide for his large family.

John was fiercely protective and treated everyone with much care and concern. I think he took a special interest in me because of my situation. During high school I was eating and sleeping at my sister's house which was a constant battle ground, otherwise I basically did whatever I wanted. In my junior and senior years I spent a lot of time at John & Sue's and they provided a welcoming home environment.

I remember John bringing in carloads of sodas for everyone. He would purchase inexpensive brands by the case and we would carry them in, case after case. I think they were 3 or 4 cents a can in bulk in those days. In their home there was always something going on with lots of Bandstand style music. John helped me to keep my car running and when I sold it for $50 and had to return the money to my sister, John somehow found me another old car.

I remember when John decided to build a swimming pool in his back yard. He hand dug a huge swimming pool size hole and lined it with a thin plastic liner. We all swam in it for quite a while until a seam broke, water went out and mud came in. Then he filled it with all his trash and unwanted items and buried it. I imagine the treasures that remain under some high tech company in Silicon Valley today.

After high school the arrangement with my sister expired and I joined the Air Force. I did well and became a missile guidance specialist. I turned 21 in Viet Nam. A day before my birthday I received a very strange message from the mail room. "Get here on the double." When I arrived there were all kinds of people waiting for me. They delivered this huge Styrofoam box about 5' long 3' wide and 1' high which I couldn't carry by myself. It turned out to be a huge cake sent by John for my birthday. He had built and sealed the box with an interior compartment that held dry ice. In the heat and humidity of Viet Nam I opened it and found the cake frozen solid. I found out later that it had become a big media event. They actually held an airplane in San Francisco for it and there was even an article in the newspaper. The cake became a real treat with my whole squadron celebrating my birthday and eating cake out in a field. Nothing like this cake could be found in Viet Nam since we normally drank powdered milk and ate powered eggs mixed with highly chlorinated water. Yuck. We used the left over dry ice to cool sodas for several days.

Later the perils and stupidity of Viet Nam finally overwhelmed me and I went to sickbay with panic attacks. I thought I was having a heart attack. They sedated me and I only vaguely remember being airlifted out of

Viet Nam. I ended up in the psych ward at the Travis AFB hospital. I must have been there for a month or two and the only visitor I had was John. I don't know how he got on base, or access to the hospital or psych ward, but John was like that. The doctors decided they couldn't fix me so I went back to work at Glasgow Air Force base in Montana for what remained of my 4 year tour.

After my military stint, John and I did many things together, along with other friends. We went shooting and hunting with bows and guns, and also did some fishing trips. One time we went shooting somewhere south of San Jose. John had a 12 gauge shotgun. I didn't see it, but someone said that a tiny rabbit jumped out of a bush. Immediately John blasted it. I think he missed because there wasn't a hair or spot to be found. Even so, we gave John a really bad time for a very long time for disintegrating a "baby rabbit." All John could do was laugh along with us.

Another time we were riding motorcycles at a huge motorcycle park, I think it was near Morgan Hill. I was hill climbing and riding through the mountains. When I returned close to where we parked John was laid out trying to recover. Someone said they were watching John ride when all of a sudden he disappeared. Actually he had crashed into a huge hole. I don't remember much after that, but later he seemed fine. He was a genuine tough guy.

So what kind of man was John? He shared his European WW2 experiences, but never mentioned his first marriage. However, Sue shared just enough to leave me with some appalling images of both of their first marriages. John had to be strong to first take on five kids alone, and then add a wife with two more; plus all their friends (like me). John was "all in" and he did life with gusto! He worked hard and played hard. He was motivated and compassionate. He was steadfast and a patriot. He lived large and spread goodness all around. However, he was not someone you would want to cross.

I call John a great man, focused and strong in a very good way. John was a man I admired, and even more, a good friend and substitute father to me. I dearly miss John & Sue. Humanity will be far less without them as the last of the "Greatest Generation" moves on to our final homes.

26. A FINAL SPIRITUAL CHALLENGE

I make my final appeal to all who read this book, and in particular, to those who are scientific minded. If we are to preserve a culture which continues to support human advancement, we cannot rely upon science alone. Ignoring human spirituality and a solid moral foundation upon which to build our lives and society is folly. How can science produce solid moral values? Why do we have kids killing each other in the streets and all sorts of other crime that is spiraling out of control? Why do we have this "if it feels good do it" mentality? Why does it seem that no one is responsible for their actions anymore? It's always someone else's fault, the way I was raised or the environment that I was in. Why are so many things that were illegal early in our history perfectly acceptable behavior now? Is there a solid source and value to morality?

The American way is to vote on issues or at least take a poll. In other words, what the majority of the people agree upon becomes acceptable behavior and eventually the law. With such a relative system, acceptable human behavior continuously expands as people become use to the ever increasing circle of acceptable activity, even after it becomes destructive to a civilized society. As soon as limits are established they are challenged by a minority of individuals. As the challenge continues and people become more numbed by the constant bombardment of the media, all limits are eventually scaled back or scrapped completely. Eventually the whole system will become unbearable for everyone and it will collapse within its own corruption.

Any society is doomed unless its members respect the system. How many people respect this system enough to not cheat on taxes, to give their employer a full eight hours and not take off a few minutes early, or to stay out of the carpool lane if the Highway Patrol are not around? For a system of government to maintain the respect of its members it must be completely worthy of respect. How can a system which allows environmental destruction in exchange for temporary gain be respected? How can a system which calls itself free and then controls what you do in, around and to your own home be respected? How can a system which claims that you have the right to own property unless you stop paying taxes be respected? No one owns anything if we must continue to pay! How can a system which establishes unreasonable laws and then uses them to unevenly tax its citizens be respected? How can a system which claims equal rights for all and then fails to provide equal educational opportunities be respected? I could go on and on but you get the picture. Unless a society can be made completely righteous and just without corruption it will not be respected and its members will do whatever they think they can get away with.

2020 Update:

How can we allow police, who are sworn to "Protect and Serve," continue to casually kill people and be completely shielded from any consequences? What law gave police the authority to become Judge, Jury and Executioner? A police person who kills someone, without an extremely justifiable cause, should be banned from all policing for life. All police should be screened and eliminated if they show even a hint of control tendencies, an elevated ego, or a lack of compassion for all. No honest person should ever feel even a little uneasy when around the police. Police should always be known for providing help in all situations! Let's create a new supportive culture within every policing situation with the motto "How may I help you?"

Without an eternal perspective, what difference does anything I do make? I will get what I can to make me feel good now, for when I'm gone nothing matters. Our society today has no answer to this desperate dilemma. Without a belief in God our lives are finite, terminal and totally desperate. On the other hand the Christian believes that he has forgiveness of sin which is given freely by a merciful God and eternal life with God if one only places faith in, and accepts Jesus as Lord of their life. Should the scientist say "this is foolishness because there is no tangible evidence that God exists and surely what cannot be physically tested does not exist"? No, God's existence cannot be proven, nor can it be disproved. As for me, I choose to live my life with purpose, confidence and the anticipation of greater things to come. Even if I am completely wrong, I have lost nothing and gained a fulfilled life.

What we need is a good old fashion revival and I am challenging the scientific community to lead the way for the sake of our country and our children's future. No, science cannot prove the existence of God, but people desperately need to believe in a creator. Where people and our government falls short, He never will. God is pure holiness and completely righteous and just. In his time he will bring justice to all injustice and correct all wrongs. He won't let you get off easy just because you can afford a better lawyer. Jesus and his teachings establish solid guidelines by which to gauge our lives. If there was a way to move our society back from the sliding average and toward fixed standards, the enormous positive effect on our society would be astounding. Just possibly all it would take to get the whole thing started is for science to say, "God is possible", even if there is no scientifically testable data beyond the documented testimony from multiple eye witnesses of Jesus, confirming all that he said and did. A lot of new scientific discoveries have less evidence than that.

Yes, I believe in an infinite multiverse and an infinite creator. Without purpose, nothing makes any sense. To study a purposeless creation leaves us empty. If everything is just an accidental machine why would it become self-aware? Left alone all machines eventually break down. Why do we constantly drive toward becoming more complex and not simply decay into less complexity?

27. LEFTOVERS

The more that I discover
The more miniscule I become

Free Dumb
Where have all our freedoms gone,
Long time passing?
Where have all our freedoms gone,
Long time ago?
Where have all our freedoms gone?
Gone to lawyers every one.
When will we ever learn?
Oh when will we....... ever learn?

Take This
A good gift comes from the heart
A great gift is one unexpected
Even greater is one undeserved

VERY LOW
For all shorty's like me
Wee will overcome

The greatest gift for a child
Is a positive belief in self

When I can no longer feast my eyes across
the seemingly endless and lush canopy of a
wild and dangerous forest, then nothing
will remain worth feasting my eyes upon.

Behold Afar
There has never been a perfect rose
But we lose our joy if we look for the flaws
Stand back and all the beauty is yours

Finding the **bad** in someone is **easy**
    Just peek inside our own hidden selves
Finding the **good** in someone is **hard**
    We must banish the pride within us

Is this Real?
If this existence is a simulation
I don't know how I could avoid
Being profoundly disappointed!

IF LOVE
You will always have someone near
To do nice things for
And gain the greatest reward
A beautiful smile

Out of Line
You may lead, but never expect me to follow
Even if a mindless ant stays in line it could not survive
Far too little sustenance falls on the beaten path

Just Do It
Complaining does nothing
Solutions come from doers
Just Like You!
Go now and do!

Entertainment is the greatest waste
Of human potential
And the most irrational
Distribution of human wealth

To seek value
At best leads nowhere

My Want and Know

There is a place where I must go
But it is never here
Where pine needle vapors fill my soul
And rushing water tickles my ears

There is a place that I need to live
Why is it never here?
Where clear mountain rivers flow
With perilous pathways from stone to stone
And peaceful places for playful deer

There is a place where I must go
Farther away with every year
A place where wild things roam
And I may gleefully skim a stone
I gaze with wonder with nothing to fear

I once knew a happy place
Gone forever now I know
Old and tired my joy replaced
All that's left is tax and moan
And I no longer remain my own

There is a place that I must find
Could it be near just out of sight?
Just beyond the fear of night
Just below the debris of life
Could finding it replace my fright?

There is a place where I must go
It has the power to guide me home
I must trample the want and crush the know
And nurture the love.... until it shows

Good bye, I need to go!

Johnny Doubter 2021

Printed in the United States
by Baker & Taylor Publisher Services